Breaking Free

Creatively Improving the Person You Are

Breaking Free

Creatively Improving the Person You Are

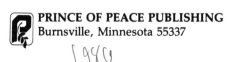

PRINCE OF PEACE PUBLISHING
Burnsville, Minnesota 55337

1980

By the Same Author:

You Can Help with Your Healing
Make Your Illness Count

Breaking Free

Unless otherwise indicated, Scripture quotations are from the Revised Standard Version of the Bible (RSV), copyrighted 1946, 1952, © 1971, 1973 by the Division of Christian Education of the National Council of Churches of Christ in the U.S.A., and are used by permission.

Library of Congress Catalog Card Number

Bittner, Vernon V.

Bibliography: p.

ISBN 0-933173-040

Printed in the United States of America

Thanksgiving Song

There is no song without the singing,
There is no gift without the bringing,
There is no life without the living,
There is no thanks without the giving.

There is no love without receiving,
There is no hope without believing,
There is no faith without the leaving,
There is no healing without the grieving.

There is no risk without the taking,
There is no change without the breaking,
There is no heart without the aching,
There is no soul without the waking.

There is no song without the singing,
There is no gift without the bringing,
There is no life without the living,
There is no thanks without the giving.

Ray Makeever

For my
Institute for Christian Living friends
who have taught me so much about love,
both human and divine

Preface

For most of my adult life I have known intellectually that love is the most *creative* force in the world. The positive results of loving and being loved are so many and so varied that I can hardly enumerate them. But the most powerful evidence of love is the transforming friendship of Christ. What makes the relationship so dynamic is His love. Without His love the relationship would not produce a lasting change. It would not be creative! Transformation is creative only when Christ's love is given . . . and received.

Unfortunately, most of my life has been spent not fully realizing the power of Christ's love. Its ability to transform one's life is overwhelming. Most of the constructive transformation that has taken place in my life has been as a result of pain, and that was followed by anger. The changes have, consequently, resulted from the *hurts* of life, not the *joys* of life. They have come because I was angry enough to change. Most of my life has been spent missing the creative transforming power of love—namely, the love of Jesus Christ communicated through the caring of other within the Christian community.

Being loved and cared for—really cared for—can transform our lives. To intellectually know the love of Christ is not enough. We have to experience it humanly. We have to touch the mind and heart of another person to know the love of Jesus.

Knowing His love takes time and a willingness to be with people who have allowed themselves to be loved by Jesus and who are willing to risk sharing His love with others. It takes our divulging all of who we are to God and others so that we can be known by them and thereby know ourselves. It takes being open enough to look at all of ourselves, even the hidden parts so that we can experience the loving friendship of Christ through the loving acceptance of others.

Breaking Free occurs only in and through relationships. If you look at the healings of Jesus, they always involved friendship. It was the power of His personal relationship that brought about a lasting change in people's lives. This has been true for me, too. However, most of the time my changes have been in spurts, because usually constructive changes have resulted from pain— not love. Consequently, the change has often not been lasting.

An example of this is that over twenty years ago I lost twenty-five pounds, and within one and a half years I gained it all back and then some. Four years ago I lost forty-five pounds and began to jog. I have with Christ's help kept those pounds off and now feel ten years younger. I am convinced that the difference has come from experiencing Christ's creative love through the personal caring friendship of the Christian community.

In this book I would like you to walk with me through my own struggle to know more fully Christ's transforming love. I want to share with you an outline for experiencing *Breaking Free*. It will give attention to the structure used in my previous book, *You Can Help with Your Healing*, which contains the "Twelve Steps for Christian Living."

Finally, in this book we will look at the three aspects necessary to make the creative process work. We will focus on our relationship with God, ourselves, and others.

Breaking Free

*"I am sure that God
who began the good work within you
will keep right on helping you grow in His grace
until His task within you is finally finished
on that day when Jesus Christ returns."*

Philippians 1:6, *The Living Bible*

Part I

God

In Part One we will look at the area of our love for God and how this is primary to our being transformed. Unless we are willing to look at our powerlessness, risk believing that Christ can transform our lives, turn our will and our lives over to Christ, and seek His discernment for our life through prayer and meditation, we cannot experience loving and being loved by our Lord. Without that LOVE experience with Jesus the Christ, we will not know the power of His transforming friendship.

*"I pray that you
will begin to understand
how incredibly great his power is
to help those who believe in him.
It is that same mighty power
that raised Christ from the dead
and seated him in the place of honor
at God's right hand in heaven."*

Ephesians 1:19-20, *The Living Bible*

Little Growth without the Loving[1]

"And Jesus said to him,
'What do you want me to do for you?'
And the blind man said to him,
'Master, let me receive my sight.'
And Jesus said to him, 'Go your way;
your faith has made you well.'
And immediately he received his sight
and followed him on the way."

Mark 10:51-52

Most of my life I have been afraid to love freely for fear of losing. Because of losses in childhood—my mother dying when I was seven, a grandmother who replaced her in the home dying a few years later, an aunt who replaced her dying a little later, and a father who relinquished his parental role—I thought the best way not to lose was not to love.

There can be a lot of hurt in loving, and there is always a risk. Many times in the past I have wondered if there wasn't a better way to live. Yet, most of my life I tried to avoid love only to experience an emptiness and a void. It is true, I didn't feel the pain of rejection, but I also didn't know the joy of loving and being loved.

There have been a lot of books written lately about self-love. Many individuals are into "doing their own thing." The emphasis

---

[1]This chapter should be read with Step I of the Twelve Steps for Christian Living: "We admit our need for God's gift of salvation, that we are powerless over certain areas of our lives and that our lives are at times sinful and unmanageable."

in our society is on being yourself and this is very important. Otherwise you lack authenticity and you appear to be superficial. But the self-love that I am speaking of here is actually *selfish* love. It is a narcissism. It is the kind of love that avoids intimacy. It is easy when you have been hurt by either the lack of love or having your love rejected, to give love up as a lost cause and opt for the god of independence. And instead of sharing that kind of love, you turn it in upon yourself.

My life was like this for almost 50 years. Protecting myself was my goal. This resulted in becoming not only a workaholic but a foodaholic as well. After all, I thought, who would have any interest in a blob, and what more admirable way to spend one's life than to "do the Lord's work as a minister of the Gospel" and be a workaholic doing it?

But independence carried to the farthest extreme brought me only loneliness and a self-destructive life. About all I gained from living that way was 45 pounds and high blood pressure. (Three years ago I lost 45 pounds, began to exercise, and I no longer have high blood pressure, but that's getting ahead of the story.)

There was growth, but it didn't last. I used independence and "doing the Lord's work" (which often was only an ego trip) as my defense. My life was made up of spurts—spurts of growth and retardation. My life was still unmanageable and I was feeling powerless to do anything about my addictions to food and work.

Little did I know that the answer to changing my lifestyle did not lie in learning how to protect myself from life. Rather the answer was in learning how to become strong enough to let a bit more of life in. I have chosen to go in this direction, and it is exhilarating!

I know that the world is full of people who feel they have to draw away into themselves. They feel they can't reach out because they are so broken that they believe they can never love again. I, too, have played the game of doing things my own way. But now, down deep inside, I am experiencing a wellspring that will not be stopped. I am saying to anyone who will listen to me, "THERE IS LITTLE GROWTH WITHOUT THE LOVING!"

I know that most of us are afraid to love—we are afraid of being hurt. Many times I have taken two steps back for every one I have taken toward someone else, even in my relationship toward the Lord. But the truth is that the moment we are most like the person God created us to be is when we reach out to God and answer His call to love Him and our neighbor as ourselves (Matthew 22:37-40). So perhaps the area of our lives in which many of us are the most powerless is in loving others and allowing God and others to love us. Maybe...just maybe this is where we are most in need of God's gift of salvation—His TRANSFORMING LOVE.

We Are All Beggars

Bartimaeus is an example of a man who reached out to Jesus. In Mark 10:46 we are told that he was blind, and being blind meant that he had a physical problem and wanted his sight back. But he was also a beggar. Often, it was the beggars who came to Jesus. This is not only true of when Jesus walked this earth, but it is also true today.

Sometimes I have wondered if there is any connection between Bartimaeus' blindness and his being a beggar. Maybe he was blind early in his life, and because he could not work he became a beggar. But, there are many blind people who do not end up being beggars.

Perhaps the real problem was that he was a beggar. Of course, it is possible that his being poor is related to his being blind, but it is hard to know which came first. Maybe it is enough to know that such a physical problem caused him to be *powerless*. Often powerlessness is a companion to poverty. Perhaps Bartimaeus' blindness (powerlessness) resulted in his not caring any more and withdrawing from the world. He had probably quit hoping. He had been so damaged by the wars of life that he had given up on himself and had begun playing the role of one who was desperate, powerless and disadvantaged. Maybe he withdrew from life because he felt rejected and

and unloved, and the way he protected himself from further hurt was by becoming a beggar.

It is true that we have to admit to our powerlessness before we realize that only God can help us—maybe even to the point of being a beggar before we are ready to reach out. But I think Bartimaeus reached out to Jesus not because he was desperate but because he had heard about Jesus and fell in love with what he had heard. And even though he was blind, he reached out. The reason I say this is because in Mark 10:48 it says that "Many of the people rebuked him, telling him to be silent." But we are then told that "He cried out all the more."

Being without the right to speak makes one even more powerless. Not only did he lack the power of sight, but the people also wanted to deny him the power of speech. If he would have been kept a beggar, you can be sure that he would have been kept blind, because beggars have no rights—they are powerless.

If, on the other hand, people are healed, they lose their powerlessness and they open up for themselves the possibility of becoming the woman or man that God created them to be. They open themselves up to salvation and God's gift of love. They open themselves up to the possibility of transformation and the abundant life.

But how does this happen? Growth requires love! Through hearing the story of Jesus, Bartimaeus experienced enough love to be courageous enough to reach out to Jesus, in spite of the rejection of the crowd. And when he did, Jesus responded by loving him and HEALING him!

You remember how it happened. There was a brief dialogue between the beggar and Jesus. He sensed that Jesus was really listening to him. Jesus says, "What do you want me to do for you?" Bartimaeus is anxious and yet concise. "Let me receive my sight."

He is telling Jesus he wants to be whole. He wants to live and be able to function. He wants his despairing dependency to end. He believes that he is entitled to more in life as a child of God, and that he can receive a better life if he only asks. All he has to do is admit to his powerlessness, be motivated by his love for Jesus, and receive Christ's transforming love.

He was healed, and so we, too, can be healed. I believe blindness comes from being a beggar. We are all beggars at times because we choose to withdraw from life instead of living it. We choose independence instead of intimacy and love. We revert back to the protective, defensive mode of living, and then life is only an existence and there is no growth, only decay.

The Tale of Two Women

I once knew two women who were slowly going blind. One was extremely wealthy. Several years before her sight began to leave her, she lost her husband. He had been her whole life. She lived for him. Wherever he went she would go. Then one day he had a massive heart attack and died.

When he died, she began to die. She stopped being socially involved. Her family tried to encourage her, but this was to no avail. This beautiful, vivacious, caring woman was slowly becoming a recluse. She sold her lovely home and moved to a lesser one. She began to mistrust people. She became so obsessed with possibly being hurt again that she didn't even go to the grocery store. All of the buying was done by others. She even put bars on her windows and doors to keep people out. She gained eighty pounds, unconsciously making sure no one would love her again. She was a millionairess, but she was a beggar. She was lost. Her life was unmanageable and it still is, as far as I know.

Then there was another woman who was losing her sight. She, too, was a beggar for a great deal of her life until one day an enormous hurt in her life was more than she could bear. She realized her powerlessness, reached down into the depths of her soul for courage, and told her Lord that she didn't want to be a "beggar" any more. She was a woman, a precious child of God, who told Him she needed His gift of love... and she received it. It changed her life. She was healed of her disease and guilt. Why? Because she reached out in love and experienced more fully than ever before His unconditional love and forgiveness. You might wonder what she is doing today. She is helping others learn to read.

Growth Requires Love

Until recently, one of my pet phrases was, "There is no growth without pain." This is true, but there is no lasting progress toward the abundant life nor consistent growth toward wholeness without love being given and received. And the greatest lover of all time was Jesus, whose love is not only indiscriminate and unconditional, but without expectations.

Right now I want you to do an exercise with me as I lead you in a guided imagery. I want you to go to your favorite chair. Put yourself in a relaxed position but stay in an alert state. If you have any tension in any part of your body, I want you to tense up that part and then relax it. Now take a few deep breaths. Breathe in through your nose and feel the breath going down into your lungs and your diaphragm. Now blow the breath out through your mouth.

You are becoming relaxed and open. Now I want you to imagine that you are blind. Try to feel what it is like to be blind. Imagine trying to walk without seeing. Are you hitting the wall or stumbling over things? How does it feel to be in a room that is completely dark? As you continue to imagine yourself blind, I want you to be at one end of a large room. Remember, you cannot see anything. Imagine that you reach down to touch the floor. Now reach over to touch the wall. What are the wall and floor like, and what kind of a room is it?

Now you can just barely hear something moving at the other end of the room. Listen carefully to the sound. You can hear a voice, but it is so soft that you cannot understand what is being said. Gradually the voice gets louder and you hear the words, "What do you want me to do for you?" From the question, you can tell that the voice belongs to Jesus and that He wants to talk to you. He wants to know why you feel powerless because He wants to transform your life from being a beggar to being His friend.

Is it resentment, greed, guilt, or loneliness? Is it alcohol, food, sex, or work? Is it diabetes, arthritis, cancer, or heart disease? What is it? You are assured that Jesus knows what you are going to say before you say it. So, you tell Him.

Then He says, "Go your way; your faith has made you well."

You are overwhelmed. How can it be that easy? And then you realize that it isn't—that this is just the beginning. You remember that after Bartimaeus' healing, he followed Jesus "on the way." The way... the way to the cross... and the way to His resurrection.

You are reminded by this that there is no growth without loving, without reaching out and being committed to love Jesus and your neighbor as well as yourself. And you are reminded that maybe, just maybe your greatest powerlessness, your greatest limitation, is not your disease, but your fear of loving and being loved, for love is really God's gift of salvation and this is what brings about healing and growth.

Lord, I used to think that growth only occurred through pain,
That there was "no gain without pain."

This IS a truism...
This IS the way my life has been...
And it HAS been productive...
It HAS been a way to achieve some goals.

But somehow, Lord, I've missed the lovin'...
And the smellin'...
I've missed the growth that lasts... that is eternal.
I've missed the abundant life.

O Lord, help me to stop being the beggar and start being
Your beautiful, worthwhile HUMAN being.
Amen.

Little Hope without the Believing[1]

" 'If I touch even his garment,
I shall be made well,'
and immediately the hemorrhage ceased;
and she felt in her body that
she was healed of her disease."

Mark 5:28-30

One of the reasons I found it so difficult to give myself in a love relationship was that I was afraid of being consumed. To really meet another and become emotionally intimate (including sharing the tough feelings like hurt, anger, guilt, fear, and loneliness, and allow myself to become vulnerable to another) is one of the most difficult tasks in the world.

Most people are unable to be consistent in this process. From time to time they instead alternate between various modes of avoidance. Some people say, "Get away from me a little closer." In most relationships, people either take on the other person's thoughts and goals, losing their own along the way, or they hold the other person at arm's length in order to protect their turf. Consequently, they close themselves off in some way and remain isolated.

Years ago people getting married planned on staying married. The emphasis was on permanency. Today many pressures are breaking up marriages. There are several reasons for running

---

[1]This chapter should be read with Step II of the Twelve Steps for Christian Living: "We come to believe through the Holy Spirit that a power who came in the person of Jesus Christ and who is greater than ourselves can transform our weaknesses into strengths."

away from love: a desire for more, boredom, wanting to be cherished, or a need to grow. The truth is that many people are afraid of love and of its hold on them, and like the alcoholic who needs "one more for the road," they believe that the next love relationship will cure them. We all need to recognize this fear and the defenses we use to avoid love. We need to realize that we are using love sometimes as a "fix," and that we will never find the abundant life this way.

Believing in Myself Has Been Hard

One thing with which I have had difficulty is believing in myself. And, of course, if you don't believe in yourself, you don't believe in others and you don't believe in God. If we lack belief in ourselves, we also have no hope, and there is LITTLE HOPE WITHOUT BELIEVING.

Lack of belief is not an uncommon phenomenon. Many people suffer from a low self-image. I remember when I was making the difficult decision to work full time with the Institute for Christian Living. When the opportunity presented itself I felt immobilized. I had difficult believing in myself, and most of all, believing that the Lord would not let me down.

The breakthrough came for me on the evening of the Ascension of our Lord. I awoke early that morning—in fact, it was 2:00 AM. I was wrestling with God. I was saying to God, "You've got to work this out...my way." And the more I wrestled, the more there was no answer.

About 5:30 AM the sun began to come up, and as it began to rise above the horizon, a light came on inside of me. I had a new realization that Jesus had not only ascended for everyone else in the world, but also for me. My heart and my soul were filled with a peace and serenity that I had not had for months. I had the assurance and the hope that somehow things would work out. Because I had come to believe the promise of our Lord, I was able to "let go and let God." I realized I wasn't afraid of how things worked out because I had the Lord with me, and that was all that mattered.

I would like to tell you that my "coming to believe" that the Lord would work things out for me was only motivated by my love for Him. However, it was also because it was difficult for me not to choose Him. And you know, it was through this process that Christ transformed my life.

Most of us have mixed motives for the changes we make in our lives. Our motives may not be pure, but what is important is whether or not we are committed to our Lord. True commitment is the result of the hope we have in Christ that transformation is possible for each one of us. For there is little hope without the believing, and it is only through our hope in Christ that transformation can occur.

Most of my life I have struggled with fear: the fear of rejection, fear of loss, fear of being wrong, even fear of life itself. Through my experience of trusting in the promise that God is always with me, I feel that Christ has delivered me from my fears and has transformed my life. Fear does not seem to be a predominant issue in my life right now because He has filled my life with hope.

I have discovered that when we give up our dependency needs to be consoled, understood, and loved, we die in a very real sense, and sometimes something new has a chance to live and grow within us. We begin to see that giving understanding and love is more important than receiving it. And if we continue in this way, we lose our unsatisfying lives and what we thought was important. For me it meant losing financial security in order to find myself. Our focus must be on Christ, for we are dependent on Him. This focus alone leads to health and wholeness. We die to the old fears and false securities, and are raised, filled with the hope which only Christ can give. We have been transformed, and weakness has been turned into strength, and fear has been replaced by hope. You see, there is LITTLE HOPE WITHOUT THE BELIEVING . . . "that a power who came in the person of Jesus Christ . . . can transform" our lives.

The Woman Who Believed

Jesus illustrates this focus in the story of the woman with the issue of blood. Some might call her impulsive and indolent because she reached out to Jesus even though she had a flow of blood—either menstrual or continual. This was rather an audacious act because women who were menstruating were considered to be unclean by the religious community. In fact, they were ostracized in rather cruel ways and kept away from the rest of society. Women were caused to feel dirty and unworthy most of their adult life when they were menstruating. This normal function was equated with uncleanness.

The most important aspect of this story, however, was that anything or anybody they touched was also considered to be unclean. Not only did the women feel like outcasts, but they were also responsible not to contaminate others.

The fact that this story is recorded in Mark and in Luke indicates its importance. Jesus wanted to make sure that even the SOCIALLY UNCLEAN would not be rejected by Him. Then, in addition, perhaps He was saying to the Jews of that day that their taboo about blood, thinking that women were dirty when they menstruated, was ridiculous.

In addition, the Mark account (Mark 5:24-34) speaks of the woman as victimized by the medical community. She "had suffered much under many physicians, and had spent all that she had, and was no better but rather grew worse." It is hard to speculate how doctors treated this problem during the first century but it is certain that she had gone every place to get help and had become progressively worse.

Obviously, the woman was desperate. She had suffered with this illness for twelve years. She had felt the abuse and rejection of one who is rejected emotionally and spiritually. Certainly a part of her reason for reaching out to Jesus was seeing Him as the last resort. She was sick and tired of being sick. Yet, I believe there was something else that was motivating her—it was hope. In spite of her physical situation and her emotional abuse, she still had HOPE that Christ would heal her, and if He did, it would transform her life.

This woman was a woman of courage, confidence and hope. She had "come to believe" that Jesus would "transform" her "weaknesses into strengths." She believed that all she would have to do is touch this man, or even His garment, and she would be made well. Sounds naive, doesn't it? But that is what she believed. She acted on her belief and she touched Jesus, and she felt herself being healed. The flow of blood stopped!

In the account, Jesus is aware that someone has touched Him because He has felt healing power go out of Him. The disciples point out to Jesus that it is impossible to discover who it was because the people were all crowded around Him. But Jesus was persistent. He wanted to know. He could have ignored it and saved face, but He had a lesson to teach through the healing that occurred.

Then the woman falls at His feet. She is trembling because she is afraid of being put down one more time. She had dared to touch Jesus who was "clean," and she was "unclean." Not only had she contaminated Jesus by touching His garment, but she had taken some of His healing power. How could she be so presumptuous?

So she grovels in the dirt before Jesus. Instead of jumping for joy, she kneels and apologizes for touching even His garment. She asks for His forgiveness for wanting to be healed and acting on this desire. I am sure the reason she did not want to be known was because she was afraid that Jesus might refuse her. But we see that Jesus loves her! Rather than condemning her, He tells her that her faith has made her whole. He knows, too, that she loves Him and believes in Him. He also knows that she is embarrassed by His singling her out in front of the crowd. In addition, He is risking His own embarrassment because He has acknowledged that He has been touched by someone who was unclean. Even so, He is willing to take a public stand against the evil taboo and state that God's love is unconditional. God's love is for everyone; it is without discrimination. Can you imagine how that must have felt for her? Her life had been transformed and her weakness could now become her strength. She could tell others what Christ had done for her.

We, Too, Are Called to Believe

Like this woman, we are all called to believe in the power of the Holy Spirit to transform our lives. Jesus desires that we believe so that our hope will help us dare to reach out to Him. He wants us to reach out to Him and be transformed from a life of disrespect, fear, and despair, to a life of self respect, belief and hope. He wants us to trust Him so that we won't hold back out of a false sense of shame and guilt, but that we will instead touch Him and use His power of love to change ourselves.

I was awakened by my own laughter at 4:30 one morning. I had had two dreams back-to-back. Not only was I laughing, but my stomach was churning, and I was feeling motivated to start writing in my journal. I immediately tried to recall my dreams because I know how important dreams are. They not only tell us what is going on in our unconscious, but also what the Lord is trying to tell us about our life and how we are to live it.

As I now recall the first dream, in it I and some others had the task of storming an enemy fort. We were to find a way to climb a high wall without a ladder. We devised a way to climb up by putting two poles together, and we all shimmied up these poles, but we stopped just before we got to the top. We wanted to remain hidden so that the enemy wouldn't discover us. But my friends were talking so loudly that I was afraid that we were all going to be discovered. And so my dream ended.

My second dream followed almost immediately. I was sitting watching a band march down the street. The drummer was way out of position. He was walking by himself and he was about ten yards away from the rest of the group, and he wasn't even keeping time with the music. He obviously wasn't living up to his potential. The conductor looked at him and waved him into the right position, and then the drummer began to beat his drums with his whole heart. He was keeping time to the music with the rest of the band. In fact, he was beating his drum so emphatically that he knocked one of the percussion men next to him off his feet. It was so funny that I began to laugh, and my laughing woke me up.

These dreams are rather ridiculous, aren't they? Well, it depends on how you look at them. To me they speak of a transformation from that of needing to hide to that of "letting it all hang out," and being what God called me to be. He wants you and me to be awakened to life and to live up to our potential, but this won't happen until we admit to our disease. For me, it has been fear, a fear of rejection. This was also the problem with the woman with the flow of blood.

Transformation or breaking through to life and "laughter" occurs at the moment we let go of our desire to have control of our lives and live in the decision that God in Christ made for all of us in His plan of salvation. For God in creation chose us to be His, and His desire for us is that we would daily live in that grace.

We can only risk believing after we have admitted that our life is unmanageable. (We are unable to work Step II until we are willing to admit our powerlessness in Step I.) We can only experience the transforming power of love revealed to us in Jesus Christ when we have admitted that we are powerless without Him.

Recognizing our powerlessness sometimes requires a painful leap toward believing. Sometimes we must leap out of a crisis. As our illusions and delusions about life and ourself begin to collapse, we look for a place to hide. And finding none we are forced to accept our weakness and our position of being powerless. Instead of listening to the beat of our own drum, we are called to be open to a new rhythm and a new direction and play this new beat with our whole heart.

Jesus tells us very clearly what we are to do: "I tell you solemnly, unless you change and become like little children you will never enter the kingdom of heaven" (Matthew 18:3). What is there about being a child? A child is filled with wonder, open to surprises, willing to risk loving and being loved, and is able to LAUGH. And most of all, a child accepts dependence upon someone else for life and safety.

A childlike attitude is the key to transformation. It is the key to a new life. Being transformed presupposes that we are willing to search for a new and exciting life in Christ. It also assumes that THERE IS LITTLE HOPE WITHOUT THE BELIEVING.

Lord, believing is sometimes so risky, and
hoping is sometimes so frustrating.

But touch us with Your love, and
fill us with Your power . . .
That our weaknesses can become our strengths.

Little Faith
without the Leaving[1]

" 'Therefore I tell you,
her sins, which are many,
are forgiven, for she loved much,
but he who is forgiven little, loves little.'
And he said to her,
'Your sins are forgiven . . .
Your faith has saved you; go in peace' "

Luke 7:47-50

Finding fulfillment for one's life has been a long search for many of us. Some people have been searching all of their lives and have never found it.

Fulfillment for me has for the most part been sporadic. I have learned to love God and myself. Where I have found myself falling short at times is in my loving of others. Loving others has mostly been on my terms, but this is not and never has been the essence of loving.

Fulfillment almost always seems to be what the other person has. We usually think that fulfillment is just around the corner, or maybe on the other side of the fence. sometimes we think fulfillment will come with becoming rich, feeling secure, or staying thin.

Most people feel that there must be more to life, but they don't really know what the "more" is, and what they thought

---

[1]This chapter should be read with Step III of the Twelve Steps for Christian Living: "We make a decision to turn our will and our lives over to the care of Christ as we understand Him — hoping to understand Him more fully."

was the answer last year may not be the answer this year. So we wait for the *Perfect Thing* that will make life complete, and we feel terrible during all the time we are *on hold*, unaware that emptiness is the result of being *in neutral*. Yes, fulfillment is difficult to find.

Be Committed

I am convinced that the answer to all of this, the key to fulfillment, is commitment: commitment to God, to others, and to ourselves. To be committed means that I place myself at the disposal of Christ and others in my life (including myself), and that I pledge myself to them and myself fundamentally. This affects not only what I have but also who and what I am.

In addition, being committed means that we are in fellowship. Commitment involves a relationship. We all, men and women, need this commitment to fellowship, not because we are strong, but because we are weak and sinful and sometimes fail in our commitments to Christ, each other, and ourselves.

Finally, commitment is unconditional. A man and a woman in marriage do not "take" each other as husband and wife under certain specified conditions. They take each other "for better, for worse; for richer, for poorer; in sickness and in health." Always the commitment is unconditional and for life. The fact that we *all* fail at times, even to the point of alienation or divorce, does not change the meaning of what we are to strive to achieve. Being a Christian is not only to believe that *He was*, but it is to believe *in Him* now with all of one's heart and mind and strength. Some might see this belief as a form of surrender and others might see it as being completely open to God and to others, as well as to ourselves and who we are.

This third step calls us to be committed to God, to make "a decision to turn our will and our lives over" to the care of God. As I am reading this step, right now at this moment, I am feeling a sense of comfort because of the word "care." The fact that God cares seems somehow to make my commitment easier. Yet, this is a difficult step for me because it means "leaving" some things. If I am really going to turn my life over to God, I am going to have to "let go" and "give up" some things because I am human and therefore a sinner. So there are going to be times when my will won't coincide with His and this requires faith, the faith to "leave" some of the things of life that block my relationship with Him. So THERE IS LITTLE FAITH WITHOUT THE LEAVING, and the leaving (of things) requires faith.

Commitment and turning our life over to God is not only what gives meaning and fulfillment to life, but it is the essence of spiritual life. "Spirituality is the response of the entire person to God who has created and preserves life, to the acceptance of God's saving love made known in Jesus Christ, and to the openness to be led by the Holy Spirit day by day.[1]

But there would be some who would say, "Isn't it enough to love God?" Scripture tells us that he who says he loves God and hates his neighbor is a liar. This means that you can't love God without loving your neighbor. And even more significant, fulfillment will not be found unless we love our neighbor AS WELL AS God.

It is not difficult to be attracted to Christ, but to really turn our will and our lives over to Him is another story. I have sometimes asked myself, "Am I really a Christian? Am I living up to the conditions of being a Christian?" Jesus left no doubt about the conditions. Those who want to follow me must put aside their own desires and conveniences and carry their cross with them every day to keep close to me!" (Luke 9:23). When Jesus invited His disciples to follow Him, He did not ask them to take up HIS cross. Rather, He challenged them to take up their OWN cross and follow Him every day of their lives.

We, like the disciples, share the same human condition, that we are sinners in need of a savior, Jesus Christ. We are also sinners who are gifted with our own strenghts and weaknesses, and this is our cross. In carrying our cross we carry with us our

---

[1]V. Bittner, Study Guide for *You Can Help With Your Healing*, p. 11.

own uniqueness. It is the person we are and the person we want to become. It is our life and even our death. Our cross is all we have been and all we hope to be in our spiritual journey with the Lord.

At times we may feel our cross is heavier than others' and that we lack the resources necessary to carry it. We may think that fate is against us and that the life situations in which we find ourselves are unfair. At other times we may even feel alone and abandoned. Paul addresses this issue and tries to assure us that no one carries their cross alone and that God will not forsake us. "The trials you have to bear are no more than people normally have. You can trust God not to let you be tried beyond your strength, and with any trial he will give you a way out of it, and the strength to bear it" (I Corinthians 10:13).

I am afraid that most of us have not fulfilled these conditions. At times our commitment is half-hearted and it becomes a commitment of convenience. Its symbol is more like that of a cushion, not a cross.

A cross! What do WE know of a cross? Often I used to think that my loneliness was a cross, or that the lack of love in my childhood was a cross. I guess that is a cross—at least for me.

But a cross is a bloody thing. Yet Jesus used the word. He used it of all who would follow Him. He tells us that we are to take up our cross and follow Him. He invites us to a friendship—a love relationship. This somehow seems contradictory. How can a bloody thing be loving? It may be both if we see love as a commitment.

I am afraid that most of us are like His disciples before the cross became real. They played at their spiritual life, and they had trouble visualizing it in the sense that it might require suffering and even death. Remember the scene at the garden of Gethsemane? The disciples were all hiding among the olive trees. Then the next day they finally came out of their hiding places to look across the valley, and the sky was strangely dark at midday. They were able to see the three crosses silhouetted against the amber sky. As they viewed the cross in the middle, these words came back to them from their unconscious memory:

"The Son of Man must suffer many things...and be crucified..."
(Matthew 16:21).

Then down the hillside they went, stumbling through the under-growth, blinded by the tears and shaking with sobs. Joined by women they climbed to the top of the dreadful Place of the Skull. They looked... Yes, it was Christ. They knelt. They never ran away again. They understood the word "cross." They realized how much the friendship which had transformed their lives might cost them. They accepted His conditions. They became Christians for the first time in their lives, at the only place a person does become a Christian, and that is at the foot of the cross. Their lives were changed. They were transformed by the creative acts of the love of Jesus Christ.

I think one of the things that holds me back from being fully committed to Jesus is that many times I am not willing to have my prayers answered. I remember praying for three years that I might work full time with the Institute for Christian Living. Then when one door closed and another opened, I was not willing to accept the opportunity because I was going to have to lose my job to make it happen. My cross was that I would have to give up the security of an excellent salary. I fought against this for three months, but finally with the help of the Holy Spirit I allowed the love of Christ to enter my life.

I experienced the "care" of Christ and I was able to let go. I realized that there was LITTLE FAITH WITHOUT THE LEAV-ING, and the leaving became possible because of Christ's care for me. I had to leave my financial security. I had to take up my cross, the part of my life in which I needed to grow, in order to really experience faith, a faith that displaces fear. Christ truly transformed my fear into faith. This happened only after I was willing to commit my life more fully to Him than I had ever experienced before.

And guess what? He didn't let me down. MY LIFE HAS BEEN SO FULL. He has graced me with His abundance. My search is over. I have found my treasure in loving Him and loving others, for this makes it possible to love myself as well.

He Loved Her First

Jesus gives us an example of this love when He encounters Simon the Pharisee. Simon was a very complacent man who felt extremely self-righteous. Simon saw no need for forgiveness, and as the story relates, he knew little about love.

Jesus is very pointed: "He who is forgiven little, loves little" (Luke 7:47). Simon was committed, but to the wrong things. He was obedient to the religious laws of that day, but he was attempting to find fulfillment through his own righteousness and he had little time for anyone else. Because he was too busy indulging himself in how well he was keeping the law, he hardly noticed either Jesus or the woman who was ministering to Him, a person known as a sinner. Simon believed that self-fulfillment through the law was what was important, not relationships.

There are many people who believe self-fulfillment ought to be our goal for life. This was true in Jesus' day, too. There is a sense in which this is true. The happiest people are those who have realized their potential. Not living up to our abilities or not recognizing our gifts can be a very destructive lifestyle because a person does not feel satisfied.

Yet, pursuing self-righteousness (rigidly keeping the commandments, for instance) for our own satisfaction is not the way to find fulfillment. It is just like trying to be happy by seeking after happiness—it is an impossible goal. Fulfillment and peace of mind do not come through searching. They come as a by-product of something else. They come because of a commitment.

There are many who would think that peace of mind comes from the absence of tension or stress. However, real fulfillment comes not from living a tensionless life, but from stretching ourselves emotionally and spiritually through the transforming love of Christ.

In contrast to Simon, who was unwilling to let go of his security in the law, the "sinful" woman was. She claimed the love, acceptance, and forgiveness of Jesus. She was willing to LEAVE her life of sin and be transformed by the loving friendship of Jesus the Christ. Her life was changed from a life of sin to a life of faith. She discovered that there was LITTLE FAITH WITH-OUT THE LEAVING, and her leaving required a faith that grew out of Christ's love.

But let us look more closely at this woman's commitment to Jesus. What was it that motivated her to love Jesus this way? Was it out of her guilt or was it out of her love? If it was only out of her guilt, I don't think she would have experienced creative transformation. In order for that to happen, she had to be loved, and she had to respond in love.

There was no doubt that she was loved. In spite of criticism by the Pharisees, Jesus loved her and He showed this by allow-ing her, a sinner, to touch Him and to wash and massage His feet, a menial task at best. Also, there is no doubt that she loved Him. Her acts of devotion and her tears express not so much penitence, but love and gratitude because she already senses that she is forgiven even before He tells her, "Your sins are for-given." It is a truism that penitence always involves love, just as one of the dynamics of love is always penitence. No person who loves ever finds that they are worthy of the love they are receiving, whether it be from God or another person. We con-tinue by faith to rely on the grace of those who love us.

This woman is both penitent and loving. She is like every other human being; her motives for responding to Jesus are mixed. The important thing is that a part of that motive is love, and even though her motive is impure, she is committed to Jesus. This is expressed not only by her leaving her life of sin but also by Jesus saying, "Your faith has saved you; go in peace" (Luke 7:48).

This story points out how important it is to be committed. It emphasizes the importance of turning our lives over to Christ and to love Him more than anything else. It clarifies beyond a doubt that faith in Christ is NOT the most important character trait of the Christian; it is loving Him. To be a Christian, loving Christ is more essential than believing in Him. However, the two go together. To love Christ is to believe in Him. But LOVE comes first. Luke does not mention "faith" until the end of the passage (verse 50). And so there is LITTLE FAITH WITHOUT THE LEAVING. I am convinced that God is love and that one can know Him only in loving, just as one can believe in Him only in loving and leaving that which was the focus of our love before our commitment to Him.

The extravagance of this woman's love—the washing of Jesus' feet with her tears, the drying of them with her hair, the kissing of His feet, the anointing of them with alabaster ointment—all of this expresses her gratitude and love. These actions seem to transcend any human expectation of loyalty and devotion which the first Christians felt for Christ. This act, as recorded in the Mark version, was a beautiful thing for she had done "what she could" (Mark 14:8). In fact, her expression of love was her way of doing everything she could to show Jesus that she loved Him. As a result, her life was transformed because she loved Jesus enough to LEAVE that which was unfulfilling, and she found a life of faith.

A Man of Faith

Some time ago I had the opportunity of knowing a man of faith. He had a high position with the church. He was looked up to by his colleagues and the people he served. Some people even put him on a pedestal. Maybe this occurred because they were unwilling to accept their part of the responsibilities within the church. After all, if he was better than they were, then he should do the work.

One day his son committed suicide. Some people talked and began to question his integrity. Others saw the suicide as part of the human predicament, that none of us is without sin. Still others knew him and knew that the way he handled the loss was through living out his faith, because he was more the consoler than the consoled to those who showed their concern.

Then one day, a year or so later, he discovered he had cancer. This man of authority realized again that he was no more exempt from illness and the reality of death than anyone else. During his time of major surgery he found himself feeling helpless and experienced the need for surrender. He spoke of having to surrender everything. Even his bowels were prepared for total surrender. As he went to sleep before the surgery, he sensed that there was no choice but to empty his hands of everything over which he thought he had control.

During the hospitalization he learned to be grateful for the smallest of blessings: a warm blanket, a hypo to relieve pain, a few chips of ice in the black of night, the first rays of light after a seemingly endless night, prayers of friends, and words of scripture from those who cared. During this time of weakness, however, he discovered an awesome sense of strength. Why? Because he was willing to surrender.

Surrender for him was victory. This is true for us as well. Surrender is not defeat. Surrendering is being able to triumph over fear because we have experienced the loving care of Christ. It is a breakthrough to freedom because we have turned "our will and our lives over to the care of Christ." Our letting go—our LEAVING the false securities behind—is actually taking a soaring leap into the center of life. At this moment we have become a faith-filled person, not because we have proven our worth, but because we have been transformed by the love of Christ and we are beginning to "understand Him more fully."

Lord, sometimes it is such a struggle to surrender.

But thank You for loving us and forgiving us
even as we struggle.
Lord, it is through Your caring that love is
created in us.
And it is through Your sharing that we can dare
to let go.
For there is little faith without the leaving . . .
and leaving requires faith.
Amen.

Little Thanks without the Giving[1]

"This, then is what I pray
kneeling before the Father, from whom every family,
whether spiritual or natural, takes its name:
out of his infinite glory, may he give you the power
through his spirit for your hidden self to grow strong,
so that Christ may live in your hearts through faith,
and then, rooted and grounded in love and built on love,
you with all the saints have strength to grasp
the breadth and the length, the height and the depth;
until knowing the love of Christ, which is beyond all knowledge,
you are filled with the utter fullness of God."

Ephesians 3:14-19, *New Jerusalem Bible*

I t it impossible to pray and meditate effectively unless we are willing to bring ourselves before God— even our hidden selves. Unless we do this we will never discover God's will for our lives, nor will we be able to act on it because our unconscious desires will get in the way.

One of the insights learned from the study of psychology is that most of our behavior is motivated by our unconscious mind. If this is true, bringing all of ourselves before God and knowing even our most hidden self is a necessary requirement to follow God's will. Prayer and meditation become the most significant way to bring this about, especially if our prayer is

---

[1]This chapter should be read with Step XI of the Twelve Steps for Christian Living: "We seek through prayer and meditation to improve our conscious contact with Christ as we understand Him, praying for knowledge of His will for us and the power to carry that out."

"Thy will be done." Then prayer and meditation become the most important way to get our will in tune with God's will.

My Fear Was Knowing Myself

When I was a high school student, I dated my childhood sweetheart, not steadily, just occasionally. I was always careful not to get too close to her, or for her to get to know me too well.

In grade school I remember giving her a May basket on the first of May. In those days we used to do that. We made them in school art class. After we had decided to whom we were going to give them, we would present them with little heart-shaped candies which had affectionate messages on them.

I remember sneaking up to her door, setting the basket down quietly, ringing the doorbell and running away so she wouldn't know who left it. I am sure she knew anyway, and later she also knew that the way I gave May baskets was symbolic of my relationship with her. I was afraid to love because she might not love me back.

When we went off to different colleges I wrote her several times but never followed through with my feelings. When I would see her at Christmas and in the summer, my heart would beat so wildly that I knew there was no hope for me if I stayed in her presence. So I would find an excuse to leave, usually that I was "too busy" to stay.

A few years after college I thought of looking her up, only to find that she had found someone else and was married.

Thirty years later, still being single, I heard that she was divorced. I resolved to look her up. Not only was I tired of living alone, but I realized that the pain of not loving was greater than facing the fear of rejection. After much searching I finally found her. I wanted to see if being in her presence would still make my heart do strange things.

I talked with her, laughed with her, and even cried with her until dawn, but the feeling didn't come back. It was gone.

On my way home, I reflected on my experience. I realized that I wasn't running away from her. I was really running away from the fear inside myself. I was afraid of seeing through her the unexplained side of myself.

The Search for Wholeness

Many people spend their lives, as I have, looking for an elusive someone special, not realizing that they are really looking for themselves. The search for the perfect other is usually the search for what we sense we lack. The reason we never find that person is that no one can make us whole but ourselves, and the way we do this is by bringing our whole self before God and experiencing more fully His unconditional love and forgiveness. Sometimes this happens through another person[1] and sometimes it happens through prayer and meditation. However, prayer and meditation are only effective when I am willing to bring even "the hidden parts before God." This is the essence of thanksgiving, for there is little thanks without the giving, even the giving of those hidden parts to God.

Learning that we are responsible for our own wholeness is a hard lesson to learn. It is difficult to stop hoping to get from others what we must provide for ourselves. It is even harder to stop waiting for God or someone else to give us what we think we need. Instead of waiting we have to look at what we can give to God and others—all that we are. This is what He wants from us and what any other mature person wants from us. Giving is the key, especially where there is little thanks. Life is joyless without the giving.

Discovering God's Will

Through the process of giving of ourselves to God in prayer and meditation, we will discover God's will for our life. However, this involves two things. First, we need to remember that God's universal will for us is to do SOMETHING LOVING WITH OUR LIVES. He wants us to glorify Him by using all the gifts He has given us. This means that we are to give all that

[1]See Chapter VI.

we are, in love. In order to fill His universal will, we need to continually ask ourselves, "What is the most loving thing to say and to do?" To be loving, to be giving, is not easy. We have to consider our own needs, the needs of others, and also the need of furthering God's kingdom on earth. This, itself, is an exercise that will promote growth and Christian maturity. In order to be loving, we need God's help. Discerning God's will is hard and we need His enlightenment. He will give us help, but He has not promised to do it for us. The final decision is ours. Growth requires that we exercise and stretch our spiritual muscles. Often we learn only by making mistakes and then altering our direction. God has given each of us the ability to think for ourselves, and when He created us all unique, He didn't have the same blueprint for everyone. We are all different and we all discover ourselves and do His will in different ways. He simply asks us to use love to structure our lives and thereby know the power of giving.

Second, we must accept that there will be times when HE IS CALLING US TO DO SOMETHING definite. Even though most of our lives will be lived following the general theme of doing the most loving thing within the scope of our sphere of influence, there will be times when He will individualize His will for us. There will be times when He will lead us to do things that only we are asked to do. No one else can do them and this is His will for us INDIVIDUALLY.

My call to be a pastor is an individualized call from God. My decision to enter the formalized ministry was difficult. It wasn't cut and dried. There were times when I thought for sure it was the thing to do, and other times when I questioned it, even to the point of attempting suicide. Ultimately, though, I knew in my heart of hearts that this was what I was called to be. I couldn't do anything else no matter how hard I tried.

There have been times when I have felt the touch of God's hand leading me in a special direction. Sometimes His desired acts of love moved me toward light and enjoyment, and other times His way was dimly lit and involved pain. But whether or not God's coming to me is affirming or frightening, consoling or confronting, I know He desires the best for me. Therefore, I must watch and pray and be ready to say "Yes" to His specially designed request even though I might not know where He is leading me.

There have also been times when I thought God was seeking me out individually, but I wasn't sure of that until after I had acted in faith. Knowing for sure what His definite will is for us is a difficult task. However, if we desire most of all to do His will and we are willing to look carefully at all of the alternatives and pick the one which gives the greatest peace to our heart and soul, we will probably find His individual will for our lives. This does not mean we might not "con" ourselves at times. Yet, if we experience an inner sense of peace, a peace of the heart, we will know that we are moving in the direction of God's will.

Peace of the heart comes from reconciling not only my conscious mind but also my unconscious mind with God's will for my life. I might have peace of mind, but I won't have peace at the core of my being unless I am doing God's will, consciously and unconsciously. This is why it is important to give all of myself to God, even the hidden parts, so that God's will becomes my will. For there is little abundance without the praying, and there is little thanks without the giving of all of me to God in prayer.

He Gave Himself to Jesus

The Grateful Samaritan in Luke 17:11-19 is the story of the ten lepers who were healed by Jesus, and about the one who returned to give thanks for his healing. This is another situation in which Jesus healed people who were considered to be social outcasts. Religiously speaking, lepers were considered unclean and untouchable. In healing these particular lepers, Jesus didn't touch them. He did, however, touch one leper at another healing (Mark 1:40-45). Jesus most likely didn't touch the lepers because they were unclean, but because their healing was not dependent upon His touching them.

The significance, however, of the story of the ten lepers was not that they were healed or even that Jesus risked being rejected by the Pharisees for touching sinful, unclean people. The significance lies in the fact that only the Samaritan was thankful. Therefore, the primary purpose of this passage is to bring to our (and the Pharisees') attention our problem of ingratitude.

In the healing experience of the leper who returned to give thanks, it is significant that there appears to be a relationship between being thankful and finding wholeness. After the leper thanks Jesus, he is told, "Rise and go your way; your faith has made you whole." It is hard to know whether this man was made whole because of his being thankful, or if he was thankful because he was made whole. Which comes first? We cannot be sure, but certainly it would be safe to say that wholeness and thankfulness go together.

Even more important is that the leper not only came to Jesus to be healed, but to "see a new thing."[1] Unfortunately, the nine lepers did not see anything or learn anything from their healing experience. In fact, they may have been worse off than before because they had an ungrateful attitude. This is a worse "leprosy" than to be physically ill.

Only the Samaritan who was an outcast was able to "see a new thing," and I believe the reason he did was because he gave all of himself to Jesus. He even gave his leprosy to Jesus; he gave his most hidden part. But what really was the part of the self that was most hidden? Was it his leprosy? I don't think so. I think it was his ingratitude.

Jesus the Christ healed his most hidden part, the part he was really the most ashamed of, his ingratitude. Thinking of the leper's suffering from leprosy most of his life and being ostracized from society, I can imagine how resentful he must have been. In fact, he probably had difficulty finding anything for which he was thankful. This is often the case with those who are suffering a debilitating disease which results in their being separated from the things and people they love.

The healing of this leper was possible not only because he was willing to give his leprosy to Jesus, but because he also

[1]Sholem Asch, *The Nazarene*.

gave Jesus his ingratitude. He was willing to share his hidden self. He came to Jesus in the most powerful attitude there is— prayer! Prayer is mostly being thankful, and prayer and meditation are more effective if we bring our whole selves before God. Our prayer can only affect our wholeness when we share our hidden self with God.

Journaling: A Method for Self Awareness

Paul's prayer on behalf of the Christians at Ephesus flows from his conviction that there is a "hidden self"—a dimension of our inward lives that can emerge into being, if with a prayerful spirit we are open to the power of the Holy Spirit. Then we will be able to gain awareness of that hidden self, know His will for our lives, and find the power to live it out in our lives.

What is this hidden self? How do we discover it? One answer to these questions lies in our willingness honestly to share ourselves with God through a life of prayer and meditation. The other answer is to share ourselves with others who are significant in our lives.[1]

As I am writing this chapter I have become aware once again of how important writing is for me, and especially the whole area of journaling. It is perhaps the most important part of my prayer and meditation life. Not only do I get into God's Word and allow it to speak to me, but writing my thoughts and feelings becomes the way that I get into myself. My writing helps me to bring all of myself before God—even the hidden parts. It is through writing that much self awareness comes to all of us. When we see ourselves on paper we realize what we are thinking or feeling or even hiding.

He Gave Himself to Others

I remember once trying to help an individual who was suffering from depression. He was a handsome man in his middle

[1]See Chapter VI.

thirties. He had a good job, a beautiful wife and three lovely children, but he was unhappy.

If you were to talk to him you would get the impression that his disappointment was coming from his job, his wife, and all of the responsibilities that go with being a parent and a father. However, if you were to spend any time at his work, observe his wife in action, and see the working of his children at home and at school, you would know that the problem lay within himself. He was the cause of his problem, and perhaps his biggest problem was ingratitude.

He had come from a middle class family. He was an only child. His parents not only had difficulty showing love, but the father was an alcoholic and the mother focused all of her attention on him. He was the recipient of all of her time and care. Whatever he wanted he would get. He even became the confidant for his mother. When things were bad between herself and her husband, she would confide in him. Because he was all she thought she had, and because she treated him as an adult instead of a child, she had difficulty refusing him anything. In his words, "She spoiled me rotten."

One can see why it was so hard for him to be grateful. He never learned it as a child. "Thank you" had never become a part of his vocabulary.

Working with him was frustrating because no matter what I suggested he refused because it wasn't on his terms. Things had always gone the way he wanted them to, or thought he did. Finally, I told him that counseling him was a waste of my time and his money.

I didn't hear from him for over a year. Then one day he called me on the telephone. I could tell from his voice that he was "up." He spoke of his new life and the happiness he had found. I experienced the joy and laughter in his voice. I asked what happened to bring about this dramatic change in his life.

At first he sounded embarrassed. "I hate to admit it," he said, "but I found a friend who was worse off than I was. Of course, that wouldn't take very much," he said, "because everything in my life was great, except me." Then he said, "What really changed me is that I tried to help him and in the process I started getting well." His healing began the moment he started giving himself to someone else. He began to find wholeness when he opened himself up and shared all of himself, even his depression and his hidden self, to this man who was in a more difficult place.

In our journey toward wholeness it is essential that we open ourselves to God at every level of our being. Opening ourselves to God can be a frightening and terrifying experience and many people avoid it out of fear and the refusal to risk the false security of the moment. Even with Jesus, only one out of ten was willing to take such a risk.

There is a temptation in all of us to choose the *status quo*. We would like to think that we have grown enough. The older we get the easier it is to think that real change is for those younger than us. We may use the excuse that we have lived longer than they and have discovered our blindness and our hidden self. After all, we do have some successes and we have achieved some of our goals. We are feeling rather secure where we are and we have been through enough failure and success, brokenness and healing. We have grown enough toward wholeness and no one will attain complete wholeness anyway until we are with our Lord in eternity.

At this point we face an important decision. We can choose to stop growing in our awareness "of Christ and His redeeming power in our life,"[1] or we can risk everything (which is no risk at all with a loving God) so that even our "hidden self can grow strong."

I believe that God's will for us is that we should continue to grow spiritually. Knowing His will and following it is really no risk at all. This, however, does not mean we will not have suffering, loneliness and pain. But the will of God is that we be happy—that we experience the abundant life. After all, this is why God created us. He wanted us to share His love, His happiness, and even His eternal home.

---

[1] Vernon J. Bittner, Study Guide for *You Can Help with Your Healing*.

As Christians we are called to continual growth. When this is our choice, prayer and meditation become a way of life. We are saying to God, "You know more about me than I do, and I want You to help me 'see new things' so that I can be open to Your will and find the power from You to act on it."

The hidden self within each of us will not emerge unless and until the false, prideful, superficial part of ourself dies. There will be little transformation or growth without putting "aside your old self," Paul writes, "which gets corrupted by following illusory desires. Your mind must be renewed by a spiritual revolution, so that you can put on the new self that has been created in God's way, in the goodness and holiness of the truth" (Ephesians 4:22-24, *Jerusalem Bible*).

The hidden self is the self in each of us that is created by loving and being loved by God. It is His love that makes our prayer with Him creative and dynamic, and it is His love that makes our meditation with Him transforming.

Through prayer and meditation the hidden self is discovered and then the hidden self is expanded, stretched, and reconciled. By bringing all of ourselves to God in prayer and meditation, we can expand our self awareness, stretch our view of our giftedness, reconcile that hidden part with the part we know, and do His will. There is little thanks without the giving. Only one returned to give thanks, and only one was made whole!

Lord, there is little healing without gratitude, and
  there is little gratitude without healing.

Lord, Your will is so unclear without the sharing.

And just as there is little following without the living,
  there is little thanks without the giving.

Lord, help us to live so that we may follow you more closely,
  so that our giving will be THANKS-GIVING.
          Amen.

Part II

Ourself

Part Two emphasizes the importance of loving oneself and how necessary self respect is for transformation to be creative and lasting. Unless we really experience this unconditional love of Christ by taking a moral inventory of ourselves, sharing all of who we are with a trusted friend, becoming open to Christ's healing, helping Christ to transform ourselves, and continuing to help in the change process by daily examining our life, we cannot experience self love. Without knowing ourself, we will not be aware of the changes that need to be made in our life. We need to begin to make these changes with Christ's help and continue to work at this process so we can grow in love and respect of ourself. To love ourself means that we need to know and be known by others, and with Christ's help those parts of our life that are destructive to ourself and to others will be healed and transformed.

*"I don't mean to say I am perfect;
I haven't learned all I should yet,
but I keep working toward that day
when I will finally be all
that Christ saved me for
and wants me to be."*

Philippians 3:12, *The Living Bible*

Little Heart without the Aching[1]

"But when he came to himself he said,
'How many of my father's hired servants
have bread and enough to spare,
but I perish here with hunger.
I will arise and go to my father . . ."
Luke 15:17-18a

Every once in awhile I awaken to the reality that I am all I've got. In the past this reality has come to me when I am feeling broken, when I'm not being the real me to others, or when the real me is not being received because others are judging, examining, or controlling me. It is at times such as this that I AM ACHING FOR THE HEART IN ME TO BE BORN.

My awareness of who I am has usually come as a result of pain. Pain can often be the motivation that a person needs to begin to look at oneself. And unless we are aware of who we are, we cannot grow spiritually. Not only are we unaware of our strengths and our giftedness, but we are blind to our weaknesses and the areas of our lives that need to be transformed. For me, discovering my true nature, my heart, requires some aching and some pain.

Every one of us born into this world represents something new, something that never existed before, something original and unique. It is your duty and mine to know that there has

[1]This chapter should be read with Step IV of the Twelve Steps for Christian Living: "We make a searching and fearless moral inventory of ourselves—both our strengths and our weaknesses."

never been anyone in the world like us. If there had been anyone like you, there would have been no need for you to be born into the world. Every one of us is new in the world, and we are called to go forth and be what God created us to be. But we cannot do it without knowing who we are, and self awareness is a lifelong process which is both exciting and at times exasperating.

Learning to know oneself on all levels is an all-consuming process. I used to think that to experience the truth about myself meant necessarily to retreat within and to engage in a process of open inquiry and meditation that would make me aware of myself. I thought this was the only way that I would be able to become who I really was supposed to be. I believed that dialoguing with myself was the only way to achieve awareness.

Self Awareness Through Dialogue

Many years ago, I intellectually learned that self awareness was also possible through dialogue with another trusted person or a small group of people. Not until recent years did I discover how powerful such dialoguing can be for one's life. I used to say that I am able to see myself as I am mirrored by others. Now I have experienced this. To share intimately with another person in a close, personal relationship is vital in knowing oneself. By this I am saying it is true that self awareness can come from spending time alone in open inquiry and meditation, but perhaps self awareness comes most of all through sharing yourself in an intimate relationship. As I have often said, "I don't know what I think; I haven't said it yet." And as the saying goes, "What a person thinks is what he or she becomes." But we don't know who we are, what we think, or what we want to become if we don't talk about it with somebody.

The Weakness of Self Doubt

One of the most devastating character defects that I have is doubting myself. I know this is true not only for me but for all of us now and then. I used to doubt myself a lot. Fortunately, I don't doubt myself very often any more, but self doubt is still an issue on which I am working.

I am aware that most of my self doubt has come from being afraid, afraid of closeness because I might get hurt. You see, most of the games we play with others have to do with avoiding confrontation with ourselves, and when you doubt yourself you doubt everyone else as well. So what is thought to be the fear of others often is really the distrust of self, just as what is usually seen as narcissism or preoccupation with self is more often the inability to love caused by a lot of self-hate.

I used to wonder why some people didn't seem to have to wait for others to accept them but asserted themselves first, while still others, no matter how much love had been squandered on them, stood begging forever at a door they had already closed.

How we feel about ourselves has a lot to do with how we were raised. There are all kinds of people who like themselves who don't have half as much to like as those who don't like themselves at all. So if we had affirming and forgiving parents we not only grew up being more self-confident, but probably also acquired more "fruits of the spirit" such as "love, joy, peace, patience, kindness, goodness, faithfulness, humility and self control" (Galatians 5:22).

Being ourselves and accepting ourselves for who we are is difficult. Unfortunately, many of us wait for others to define who we are, or we wait for others to give us permission to be what we have always been.

In actuality, we are all who we are by courtesy of someone else, and since we need others to see ourselves as we really are and to experience who we are, it is extremely important to be in affirming relationships.

For example, it is very hard to like yourself when those nearest you seem to doubt your value. In addition, it is also important that those closest to you are willing and able to honestly confront you in a loving way about those character traits that are destructive to you. Becoming the person that God created you to be requires affirmation, and creatively transforming one's defects of character involves loving confrontation. For there is LITTLE HEART WITHOUT THE ACHING, and one does not discover one's true nature without the comfort and even discomfort of truly being loved.

We all wear so many faces assuming our true identity is very hard to do. The fact is that most of us are "wired." We have all kinds of wires connected to us, especially those we don't see. There are the wires of guilt, resentment, vanity and fear which we make for ourselves, and there are the wires of other people's expectations. But perhaps the wire that most strangles us is the myth that some people like to put on us, and if we aren't alert enough to sidestep such controlling people we can live out our whole life being what *they* say we are.

There are some people who think that to love and accept yourself is being proud. I cannot accept that premise, because usually accepting oneself is feeling secure, but being proud is a sign of insecurity. When you have a healthy sense of self-pride you don't have to put on false airs. You accept yourself as you are and expect others to do the same. When you lack self worth and are afraid to be yourself, you place yourself in a very vulnerable position. You give away your power to others and they have control over you. None of us needs to constantly please others to be loved. If the people in our life only love us when we wear the face they like, they don't really love us. We need to be ourselves and if we are not loved for this, we haven't lost much.

He Discovered Himself

The story of the Prodigal Son in Luke 15:11-24 is an example of how important it is to discover our true nature and the real "heart" of our being. It is a story of a person who finally "came to himself" and decided to claim his birthright and be what God had intended him to be. It is an account of a man who used his self awareness to change his life.

Actually, every one of us is the Prodigal and wherever we are is the "far country," because all of us who are working on our spiritual growth are continually COMING TO OURSELVES from a life that is self destructive. This is what it means to be human.

The Prodigal was like many of us who go through a stage of rebellion and who think freedom is irresponsibility. The Prodigal was a person who was preoccupied with himself. He didn't have any time to think about his father or brother or even his mother. His only thought was of himself. His selfishness, which was really self-hatred, brought him to a place far from home. Because he had turned away from God and his own family and was living a destructive life, even more despiteful things happened to him. He had isolated himself from the people who loved him and even his so-called friends deserted him. They were takers, not givers. Finally, his self-created pigpen became so distasteful that he began to think about home. His pain and loneliness helped him to see himself for what he was. His ACH-ING caused him to see where his HEART really was—it was to go home and to be a son.

Self awareness is always the beginning of spiritual growth and transformation. The Prodigal, however, came to himself not only because of his pain, but also because of the unconditional love of his father that he knew would be there when he returned. This is what made his transformation so creative—he knew he was loved and so he was able to believe in love and repentance.

The Prodigal had been asleep to himself. He had deluded himself into thinking he was living his "real life." He realized that such a life was not life at all. With no joy, no friends, no inner peace, it had become a death—a slow death. It is the kind of existence that many of us live from time to time. He had fallen so far from life that he had more in common with pigs than with humans.

Be Yourself

I am impressed with the optimism of Jesus as He told this story, and I am struck by His urgency. His words, "When he came to himself," speak of His compassion for us. Jesus sees so many of us choose not to be who we are. Jesus sees the real you—the real me—and I think He would like to say, "Be yourself!"

We can say to a chair, "Be a chair," or to a dog, "Be a dog," because chairs and dogs have no choice. But you and I have a choice. And within each of us there is a war going on between the real and the unreal. And there is an "aching" for the "heart" in each of us to be born. "When he came to himself" he turned homeward, which was the will of his father. And the will of our father/mother God is that we truly know and become ourselves.

I once met a man who was in love with a warm and tender woman. He loved her very deeply and she loved him as well. There was only one problem—she was already married. They would see each other secretly. Much of their relationship was on the telephone. They developed the kind of emotional intimacy that most people never have in marriage.

Then one day his beloved discovered that she was pregnant by her husband. This man found himself becoming very jealous. This happening was a revelation to him that she was not his alone. He tormented himself with thoughts of her being with her husband. The more he ruminated about this, the more fearful he became. Soon his fear turned to distrust. He thought, if she can be with her husband and still tell me she loves me, who else could she be with?

He told a friend his dilemma. He talked about his fears and his suspicions. He spoke of his sleepless nights and how he was overwhelmed by thoughts that she might have other loves as well as himself.

His friend laughed at him and assured him that he had the best of both worlds. "After all," he said, "you have the love of a beautiful woman without the responsibilities of being a husband and a provider."

In spite of the words of his friend, he became more and more depressed. Finally, his friend suggested a way to help him out. "I'll call her and ask her for a date and see what she does. This will take away your fear," he said. So the man agreed to have his friend do that and he thanked him for his help.

After that I never heard from this man again and I never did find out what happened. But less than a year later I was in a grocery store and met an old acquaintance there. We began to talk. He spoke of this man and told me that he had heard he had died a month earlier. Apparently he died from a self-inflicted bullet wound to the head.

Since then I have thought of him again. I wish he hadn't died. Every time I think of him it comes to me that we are all a little like him in that we often so fear being rejected that we reject ourselves first, before anyone else has a chance to reject us.

Being afraid to know ourselves and be ourselves is an issue with which we all struggle. Some of us are better at it than others. Yet, what makes it possible for us to be our true selves is the promise that no matter what we discover about ourself it will never be so bad that the Lord won't love us and forgive us.

This love and forgiveness gives us courage to take a "fearless moral inventory of ourselves." Because God loves us unconditionally, we are able to find the motivation to know our true nature. For there is no possibility of really being who we are without the comfort and discomfort of truly being loved. So, too, there is LITTLE HEART WITHOUT THE ACHING.

Lord, You who accepts us unconditionally and just as we are,
Give us caring . . . to see;
Give us wisdom . . . to know; and
Give us courage . . . to be . . .
So that through our ACHING, the HEART in all of us
will be born.
Amen.

Little Risk without the Taking[1]

"Jesus looked up and said to her,
'Woman, where are they?
Has no one condemned you?'
She said, 'No one, Lord.'
And Jesus said, 'Neither do I condemn you;
go, and do not sin again.' "

John 8:10-11

"The transformation of our lives would be impossible unless we were willing to break with the sins of the past."[2] Therefore, the motivation for allowing Christ to help us change our lives comes from the experience of sharing all of ourselves with a trusted friend.

One of the most important steps in learning to love and respect oneself is allowing that self to be vulnerable, not only to oneself and Christ, but also to a trusted friend, spouse, pastor, or spiritual guide.[3] This involves not only sharing the sins of the past that are weighing me down, but my giftedness as well.

Christian growth and transformation involve loving myself, as well as God and others. The primary way that this is accomplished is through self awareness (Step IV), sharing myself with Christ (Step XI), and sharing myself with a trusted friend (Step V), the aspect that I will discuss in this chapter.

---

[1] This chapter should be read with Step V of the Twelve Steps for Christian Living: "We admit to Christ, to ourselves, and to another human being the exact nature of our sins."
[2] V. Bittner, "Study Guide," *You Can Help with Your Healing*, p. 14.
[3] "Friend, spouse, pastor, or spiritual guide" will hereafter be "FRIEND."

We cannot come to our full potential until we love ourselves as God has loved us through Christ. Loving ourselves is not possible by our own actions alone. It happens as we allow the divine love of Christ to move in and through us and transform us into becoming what God created us to be. This love, however, is most often experienced through other human beings and will only happen as we allow others to really know us as our innermost selves. Their loving us is only made possible by their knowing us, and their knowing us requires that we allow ourselves to be vulnerable people. For there is little loving without the knowing, and there is LITTLE RISK WITHOUT THE TAKING.

I Need at Least Two Soulmates

There are a lot of people who spend too much of their time trying to control others. There are people who try to control others out of fear, and still others who do it for the "fun" of having power. Getting control over others has a lot to do with making them weak. The theory is that if someone is indebted to you, they are in an impotent position.

I used to think that confessing who I was (all of myself) to someone else would put me in a dependent position. Instead, however, I have discovered that confession becomes an affirmation when it is done with a loving and trusted friend. In fact, I have gained in self awareness, self understanding, and self affirmation when I make myself vulnerable through confession. Confession to a trusted friend gives me power. Instead of being controlled by forces within or without, this act of confession puts me in a position to take control of my own life.

I also used to think if I could find the one perfect person with whom to share my life, I wouldn't need anyone else. I know now that there is no one person (besides Christ) who can fulfill all of our needs. We need more than one friend, but we do need at least one person besides Christ in whom to confide and who will allow us to be our true selves. Ideally, this person will be both a friend and a lover—our spouse, or in some cases our important other.

There are many Christian psychotherapists (including myself) who feel there is a direct relationship between our self-disclosure and our spiritual and emotional health. The more open a person is, the healthier he or she is emotionally and spiritually. Not only does this person have closer friends, but this person will probably live longer because he/she is more honest. Being honest and admitting our strengths and weaknesses is not only necessary for knowing and loving ourself, but also to maintain our own physical health.

There are some who use the excuse that revealing yourself to Christ and to another human being robs you of dignity. But there is no dignity in pretending to be something other than what you are. We all need at least one person with whom we can be ourselves. In this relationship we feel acceptance and find the courage to risk ourselves with even more people. When we pretend to be somebody other than the person we are, our estrangement from ourselves keeps others away from us as well. In time, alienation becomes a way of life and is so automatic that we do it unknowingly.

Loving involves trust, and trusting involves the TAKING OF A RISK. The people we love are the people we trust, and the people we trust are the people with whom we are willing to take a risk. If we are unwilling to take a risk, we are unwilling to love and be loved. And the person we need to take a risk with most of all is God. This risk allows us to learn to love ourselves.

When we wear a false front, we are saying, "I don't trust you." The real reason we don't let trusted friends see us as we see ourselves is not that we don't like them, but because we don't love ourselves. Yet, the message we often communicate is that we don't love or trust them.

It is significant that the problem is the solution. The reason we avoid taking the risk of sharing ourselves is because we don't have enough self-love. The way we learn to love ourselves is by being ourselves with others so that they can know us, and so we can understand that they are loving us because they indeed know us.

It is almost impossible to experience being loved if I haven't risked being the person I know myself to be with a trusted friend. There is little experience of love without being known, and there is little act of risk without it being taken. Loving oneself involves being known by a trusted friend, and through the dynamic of that loving and creative relationship, learning even MORE FULLY TO KNOW MYSELF.

In other words, knowing and loving oneself results not only from being myself with a trusted friend, but learning even more about myself through the process of confession.

Jesus Did Not Condemn Her

The account of Jesus and the woman taken in adultery in Mark 8:1-11 illustrates vividly how a person is able to more fully love herself through the process of confession. Through sharing herself with Jesus and experiencing His love and forgiveness, she grew in her ability to know and love herself.

In this story a woman is brought before Jesus for His judgment. Scripture says that she has been "caught" in the act of adultery. The Pharisees remind Jesus that such a woman is to be stoned according to Jewish law. They want to put Jesus to the test and see if they can't get Him to trip Himself up and say the wrong thing.

There might be some discerning women reading this account who would be amused. After all, how could a woman be "caught" in the act of adultery without a man being caught as well. It does take at least two people to commit adultery. This biased attitude not only existed in Jesus' day, but also exists today. Somehow in both societies men are regarded as less guilty in sexual sins than women.

Thankfully, things are changing somewhat today. For example, it used to be that only the woman who worked as a prostitute was arrested for breaking the law. Today many police departments are also arresting the man who is patronizing a prostitute.

Yet, it is obvious that Jesus understood that the man was as guilty as the woman. He knew that adultery was not exclusively a woman's sin, and decided to show the men their guilt.

This was a big risk for Jesus, but He felt it was worth the taking. Not only did He have to face a group of Pharisees, but a crowd had gathered and they were ready to witness the testing of Jesus.

You can imagine the intensity of the scene. Jesus was put on the spot in front of people who loved and respected Him. They waited. What would Jesus do? Would He be the first to throw a rock? Wasn't He also trained to see the sin of sex to be only the woman's and not the man's?

Jesus leans down. He writes something in the sand. We are not told what He wrote. Did He write down the name of the man?

Whatever He wrote, we can be sure that it was relevant. Nothing He did was without meaning. Perhaps we can assume it had something to do with the situation of adultery. The crowd not only knew the laws, but they also knew the double standard for men. They knew that women were punished and men were only admonished for adultery.

Then Jesus says, "Let him who is without sin among you be the first to throw a stone at her." Some might say that Jesus is only saying that we are all sinners. Certainly He is saying this, but more importantly He is saying that men are guilty, too, of sexual sins. Adultery takes two!

We are told that the Pharisees and the crowd all began to leave after Jesus said this. They knew that men are as guilty as women. Then Jesus asks, "'Does no one condemn you?' She says, 'No one, Lord.' and Jesus said, 'Neither do I condemn you; go and do not sin again.'"

These last two statements of Jesus are the climax of the scene. Not only does Jesus tell her to sin no more, but He refuses to condemn her. Christians have heard that she was to "go and sin no more," but many of us have missed the message He does not condemn her. Through this confession and dialogue Jesus uncovers her real sin — SELF CONDEMNATION. Not that the sin of adultery is unimportant, but if it would have been the most important sin He would have admonished her. But He didn't. He said He wouldn't judge her for that sin, but rather only for the sin of self condemnation.

Jesus is telling her, "What you really need, my precious daughter, is not to be reminded of your adultery, but to stop condemning yourself. To show you how important that is, I will not condemn you." Instead of giving a negative judgment, Jesus gave her a positive one.

Interestingly, Jesus did not say the same to the men, because they needed to face their sin. That is why Jesus says that harlots will get into the Kingdom before Pharisees. The men left, but He didn't tell them that He wouldn't condemn them.

Does this mean that there is no guilt for sexual sin? Certainly not! Jesus calls it a sin, for He says, "Go and sin no more," but He doesn't condemn it. Rather, He forgives it! The sin of self condemnation and of self righteousness is the sin that Jesus condemns.

Why have we as Christians missed this message? Would this give people too much freedom? Would they not sin too freely if they knew there would be no condemnation? If grace is free, then why not sin boldly so that grace may abound?

Even Paul had difficulty with this. He said that Christians were above the law but he established many rules for Christian behavior. Didn't he trust the followers of Christ of that day? I don't know the mind of Paul, but he said there is no need of laws for those who possess the love of Christ. "Love does no wrong to a neighbor; therefore, love is the fulfilling of the law" (Romans 13:10).

But some would say, if there is no condemnation of this sin, how can people be kept in line? Maybe if sexual sin is not only the guilt of women, it might be possible for men to learn responsibility for their conduct. How can people be convinced to behave?

The obvious answer is by experiencing the love and unconditional forgiveness of God revealed through Jesus Christ. It is only possible for men and women to live a morally ethical life when they have experienced the abundant life. Moral living that lasts comes from joy and gratitude to God. Fear of punishment, rejection, and condemnation will never transform our lives. Transformation — creative transformation — comes from having been loved divinely and humanly. This love is the result of allowing oneself to be known. Just as there is little love without the knowing — there is LITTLE RISK WITHOUT THE TAKING.

How to Love Ourselves

Working the Fifth Step is primary in learning to love oneself. Unless I am willing to bring all of myself to a trusted friend, I will have difficulty experiencing love and respect for myself. There are certain things that could help us to get to the place of taking this risk.

First, we must imagine ourselves as seen through the eyes of the Perfect Lover — Jesus Christ. In order to work on this, I would suggest that you consider keeping a journal if you are not already doing so. It is difficult to reflect in depth on the love Christ has for me, so to keep from going over the same ground again and again it will help to keep track of our progress toward self-love. This could also help us to look at why we have such a difficult time loving ourselves.

Second, in order to love ourselves we must be honest with ourselves. In my experience of counseling I often see people judging themselves for the wrong mistakes and attitudes. Many people feel guilty for the wrong things. Often sexual sins are considered far worse than the sins of pride, arrogance, and self righteousness. Unless I look at myself objectively, it will be difficult to see what is good and what I need to change. There is no need to seek forgiveness for behavior in which we need no forgiveness. We need to distinguish between sin and shame.

Third, in order to accept ourselves we must realize that we need some help beyond ourselves in order to experience self-love. It is not enough to intellectually know God's love; I have to experience it on a human level. This means that I need to go to a trusted friend and share all of who I am and become known so that I can be loved. This way I will experience more fully God's love.

Finally, we must accept the forgiveness of others. It is easier for many of us to forgive others than it is to be forgiven. This is why confessing who we are to another person in whom we can trust is so important. It is almost impossible to come to self-love unless we allow ourselves to be known by someone else without holding anything back. Only then can we realize that they can love us and forgive us in spite of and because of who we are. Then it becomes easier to accept forgiveness from others and to love ourselves.

Control Is Not the Answer

I once had the opportunity of working with a man whose wife had been unfaithful. He was very hurt and disgusted because of what she had done. He felt put upon and throughout the marriage counseling he was trying to put the blame on her. He was saying in effect, "If she would just get her act together, everything would be all right."

Significantly, he said he had "found Christ" through the faith of his wife. When they first got married he was a very selfish and controlling man. After his spiritual experience he managed to get rid of some of his selfishness, but now he was camouflaging his need for control by claiming to be Christian. He really hadn't changed his greatest sin of trying to control his wife, and doing this by putting her down with a self-righteous attitude.

As a result, his wife felt unloved. The only place she felt any sense of worth was at work. She worked long hours and eventually got involved with someone at work.

Her husband was appalled. Wasn't that adultery? Shouldn't she repent and come back into the marriage? She might admit to wrongs which she did, but she was afraid that he was not going to change. He would still be barking orders at her like the captain of a ship, and she would probably fall right back into her old pattern of scurrying around and carrying out his bidding as if she were a maid.

She refused to be bullied. She told him she wouldn't come back and that she wanted out of the marriage. When his attempt to control his wife didn't work, he tried to guilt me into shaming her in order to control her. When I refused to go along with this ploy, he accused me of promoting divorce. Then he went to the pastor of his church and tried to get him to guilt her. And when that didn't work he began to talk to people he knew to get them to call me to "shape up and be a 'Christian' counselor."

As far as I know, he is still trying to control others and is still self-righteously condemning those who don't agree with him. His wife has filed for divorce. He had won in the sense that he hadn't looked at his own sin, but he had lost not only his wife but also any peace of heart he could have had from doing God's will.[1]

Transformation is impossible without breaking with the sins of the past. For him it was his need to control someone else and transfer the blame from himself to others through his self-righteous attitude. It was not enough for him to confess his sin to himself and to God (and I don't know if he even did that). It is also necessary to confess one's sins to a trusted friend. Perhaps the most trusted friend he had was his wife who had been both his friend and lover for years.

The experience of self-love is limited without bringing all of myself/ yourself to be known by a trusted friend. There is LITTLE RISK WITHOUT THE TAKING.

Lord, so long I have thought of myself as condemned.

I have been controlled by my shame . . .
 Unwilling to see myself through a lover's kind
  and patient eyes.
 Unwilling to see myself honestly,
 Unwilling to see I needed someone beyond myself,
 Unwilling to see Your forgiveness was real.

[1]See Chapter IV.

Thank You, though, for loving me and forgiving me.
  And thank You for sending a trusted friend
    to make that love real.
  And thank You, too, for the courage to be willing
    to be known.

For there is no experience of love without being known,
  And there is LITTLE RISK WITHOUT THE TAKING.
    Amen.

Little Change without the Breaking[1]

*"And there was a woman who had
had a spirit of infirmity for eighteen years;
she was bent over and could not fully straighten herself.
And when Jesus saw her, he called her and said to her,
'Woman, you are freed from your infirmity.'
And he laid his hands upon her,
and immediately she was made straight,
and she praised God."*

Luke 13:11-13 (Luke 13:10-17)

We are powerless to change things "without the help of Christ."[2] Until we have worked on Step V and have broken with the sins of the past and become aware of our positive character traits, we are not open to allowing Christ to help us change what we need to change. Neither are we able to build on our strengths and use them to make the needed changes.

When I think of myself as a child growing up, I am aware of having learned two life scripts very well. They were to please others and to work hard. Thinking back on my life, I realize that they were the primary values for my life and have molded me into being the person I am now. I will deal with the concept of

---

[1]This chapter should be read with Step VI of the Twelve Steps for Christian Living: "We become entirely ready to have Christ heal all of these defects of character that prevent us from having a more spiritual lifestyle."

[2]V. Bittner, "Study Guide," *You Can Help with Your Healing*, p. 15.

pleasing others in this chapter and will deal with the concept of working hard in Chapter VIII.

Motivation for Change

Both of these values were positive for me in that they helped me achieve some of the "success" in my life. However, pleasing others has helped me to attempt to be all things to all people, which often in the past meant that I was NOBODY to EVERY-BODY. No one really got to know me. Oh, I would let them in a little bit, but it was usually on my terms. I would let them know me, just enough to get what I wanted and that was all. As I am writing this, I know I am being hard on myself and am exaggerating to some degree, but this behavior was my pattern for living in many situations.

In high school, I was into everything. As a senior I received not only the highest award for music, but for athletics as well. Of course, there were only thirty-six in my class, but I did go on to excel in both activities in college and beyond.

I was a "success"...or was I? I certainly pleased a lot of people. Most people thought I was nice, but I'm sure some people thought I was too good to be real, and I was. They just didn't know me. No one really knew me. I was too busy pleasing too many people.

Most of my life I was so busy pleasing others that I forgot to please myself. The way I lived was to be what I thought others wanted me to be. I was always good, and at times I felt sick of being good! — especially when I realized how I had cheated myself throughout the years. Besides, nice guys get walked on a lot.

Being a people pleaser has had one other drawback, and that is that I have spent most of my life without any real friends. Oh, I have had a lot of acquaintances, because people pleasers are good at that. In high school, I really never "hung around" with any of the guys that much. I was too busy pleasing, and it seemed that the more I tried to please, the less I felt close to any of my classmates. This was also true in college. It seemed that the more I did for others the more isolated I felt. Perhaps it was because they were threatened by my achievements, and the message they picked up from my people pleasing was that I thought I was better than they.

There was one person, I remember, whose approval I wanted very much. Every time I saw him I would try to please him with what I had accomplished. But the harder I tried the less inclined he was to accept me. No matter how hard I tried I never got his approval.

Years later I realized what had happened between us. I became aware of his need to have my approval while all the time I was seeking his. When I figured this out, it was too late for both of us. At that moment I decided that the best way to let anyone know that you accept them is to let them know you and show them that you need them.

This experience taught me that others have needs as great as mine. Unfortunately, we are all so involved in ourselves that we fail to realize others have needs to be fed and nurtured just as we do — that they are hurting, shy, and feeling broken and need someone to reach out to them.

At this stage of my life I am "entirely ready to have Christ heal" this defect of character that prevents me "from having a more spiritual lifestyle."[1] I only hope and pray that the Lord will continue to help me to be open to His healing, not only for my people pleasing, but for all of the areas of my life that are in need of His healing and transformation. For there is little change without the breaking, breaking destructive old habits.

I believe that Christ is healing my destructive habit patterns by helping me to bring all of myself to some of the important others in my life. He is showing me that this is the most satisfying way of life — to be a friend and to be befriended. Besides this, He is showing me that a positive character trait of this lifestyle is that I am a lover and not a fighter!

---

[1]"You will note that I have changed this sixth step from the original from "remove" to "heal." We can usually never even with Christ's help remove all of our shortcomings, but Christ can heal them so that they do not have a destructive influence on our lives.

For many people life is like an all-out war. Each side is waiting for the other side to put their guns down first, and just to carry arms of any kind is likely to result in your being shot at. A lot of people are fighting against life. Instead of letting life in, they are shutting it out.

The greatest "success" that I have experienced is to stop shutting out life! By being the lover I really am, I am risking all of who I am with some trusted friends and I am experiencing the abundant life as a result. I don't need the rigidity of pleasing others to be a moral person. Now my Christian values are coming from my joy and gratitude to God for what He through Christ has done and is doing for me. He is truly healing me!

If I were asked which life script—Be good, Be perfect, Be strong, Work hard, or Please others—would be the best for me to have, I would say none of them and all of them at the same time. Whatever your life script is, you would do best to put down your weapons and fears and take the risk of being all that you are with at least one trusted friend besides your Lord. This would not only be fulfilling for you but it would also help you to "become entirely ready to have Christ heal" all of these defects of character that you have. The Lord isn't finished with any of us, yet!

She Was Ready to Be Healed

The story of the freed woman is a dramatic account of how Jesus sees everyone as important and of how He seeks us out because He knows our desires and our helplessness. He wants to heal us.

The setting is in the synagogue which had an ordinance that women not enter the area that was considered holy. So when Jesus calls this woman to Him, He may already be breaking a rule.

It is interesting that Jesus didn't hesitate. He didn't wait for her to call to Him because He realized that she could not see Him. She was bent over. Yet, He knew what was in her heart.

She had been this way for eighteen years and she was ready to have Him heal her of her disease.

As Jesus looked at this woman He felt compassion for her. He didn't ask for her life story or even her medical history. He didn't even do an "intake interview" on her. He simply saw a woman who was crippled, and then He acted. He didn't discuss her morals. Instead, He spoke directly to her need. "Woman, you are freed."

In this passage we are not told what her "infirmity" was, but apparently it was known by all of the people who were present. Otherwise, He would have named it. What is significant about all of the healings of Jesus is that He was always desirous of a spiritual healing as well as a physical one.

What was causing her to be bent over? Was it that she was weighed down with all of life's burdens? Did she have an inferiority complex? Was she afraid of rejection so that she isolated herself by looking at the ground? Or was she trying to please people by being subordinate to them, thinking she had no rights of her own?

Whatever her problem was, Jesus freed her. He told her that whatever it was that was binding her or bending her, He was now healing. "You are free!"

Then the Savior and the bent woman touch. He frees her before He touches her. He heals her spiritually from whatever character defect she has had because after eighteen years she is finally ready to be healed. Some people wait a lifetime and never become ready to be healed by Christ. He touches her and confirms her spiritual healing by healing her body.

The fact that Jesus touches her is significant. She might have had a communicable disease. She could even have had lice, leprosy, or a veneral disease. Yet, He touches her—a woman who is considered to be unclean by any Jewish male. And she is made straight. Imagine her body being stretched out, and her spirit is stretched as well.

Can you imagine the people staring at her as her body is changing by the healing power of Christ's love? I would guess her face and her whole being were glowing with the transformation that took place.

Significantly, she doesn't disappear into the crowd. Instead she acts. There is no hesitation. She knows what has happened. She has been healed within and without. She praises God. She is grateful for her healing, so she is healed spiritually as well. Remember the nine lepers who gave no thanks. They were probably only healed physically and therefore were not able to give thanks. They were not entirely ready to be healed of their greatest sin—ingratitude, whereas this woman was ready for Christ to heal her... ENTIRELY.

One wonders what was meant by her "praising God." The King James version says she "glorified God." Obviously she must have begun a NEW life. After all, she was healed, and so she probably told people her story. After all, this is the best Christian witness we can give and it is also an important factor in our continuing to grow as Christians. We need to tell our story of how Christ has healed us and how He is transforming our life by His love.

I am sure she couldn't keep her healing to herself. After taking eighteen years to become ready to have Christ heal her, she probably couldn't stop talking about it. Yes, she couldn't restrain herself; she praised God. Out of her joy and gratitude to God, she became an instant missionary for the ministry of Jesus. Not only was she healed, but her whole life was changed. She was finally able to stand straight and look people in the eye because she had been healed of her spiritual disease, and this resulted in her ability to respect herself. She was now able to "stand tall." She had experienced the dynamic love of Christ and her life had been transformed. She was willing to break from her disease and be changed by Christ, for there is little change without the breaking, breaking with the burden of the past that bent her over.

Change Is Hard

Self-love is hard to come by. Yet, we are called by Christ to love ourselves. Not loving ourselves is a malady that all people suffer from at one time or another. The behavior that tends to reinforce these negative feelings about ourselves is failing to change that part of ourselves that is destructive and for which we dislike ourselves. There are two reasons why it is so hard to become entirely ready.

First, there is a security in holding onto that which is familiar. Even though this behavior may be painful, we know what to expect. It is predictable. If we change, we don't know what will happen. Besides, as the saying goes, "Bad habits are like living organisms; they die hard."

Second, becoming ready to change is so hard because our pride blocks us. After all, who wants to be dependent? None of us wants to be accused of being irresponsible. Besides, we want to heal ourselves, because we want to be healed OUR WAY.

Unfortunately or fortunately, this is usually not the way true healing works. Many times God's way is not on MY TERMS or in MY TIME. If we expect Christ to heal us, because we can't heal ourselves, we only have to be ready. No matter how much we would like to be healed, we can't tell Him how or when to do it, because He knows best. In the same sense we don't tell a doctor how to treat us because this has not been our training.

Most of us find change hard. We all feel resistant to change at times. There is a beast in all of us that will not allow us to become vulnerable enough to allow change. I am not sure why we feel so fragile and why so many of us go through life like wounded animals waiting for someone to attack us. When we are in this frame of mind, an attack usually happens. It is almost like we bring it on ourselves by expecting it. For if we expect it long enough, we will probably do something inadvertently to make it happen, just because others are as frightened as we are.

I know that I used to feel that closing myself off from myself and others would free me. The story of the freed woman shoots that theory. Unless we are open to Christ and to ourselves we will find little freedom, even the freedom to be open to others.

He Broke with His Past

They were having difficulty in their marriage. This, at least, was the surface reason for their coming in to see me. They were both in their middle thirties. They had three children. Things were at the point where nothing was very meaningful any more in their marriage. Initially they stated that the problem was communication. This is always a safe place in which to start. Most people have trouble communicating at one time or another and most of us could learn more about communication. However, many times there is a reason why communication is being blocked.

At the second meeting, the wife found enough courage to talk about her husband's drinking. During that session he was able to admit that he had a drinking problem, because when he drank he had problems. I encouraged him to go to Alcoholics Anonymous, and I told his wife she needed to go to Al-Anon. I told them both that unless he was willing to stop drinking I would not be able to help them with their marriage problem. For there is little change without the breaking, and for him he was going to have to break his drinking pattern.

He was able to control his drinking by going to Alcoholics Anonymous. At first he went almost every day, but eventually it was only twice a week. We had agreed that he would go to treatment if he wasn't able to abstain completely on his own with the help of Alcoholics Anonymous. As he began to straighten out his thinking, he became more and more aware of his real problem, which was his fear of intimacy. Alcohol was his way to hide from being close and also the stimulus he needed to even be a little bit close with his wife.

Interestingly, fear of intimacy was his wife's problem as well. This is often the case. That is why they found each other. If either one of them had wanted to be closer emotionally, they would have found someone else. Now that he was working on being close, she would have to do it, too. He was willing to have Christ change his life from that of being afraid of closeness to craving it.

The husband was making great strides in his progress. However, it seemed that she became more closed as he became more open. Christ was healing him, but she was still hanging on to her anger for what he had done while he was drinking. Her anger protected her from risking intimacy. Unless she could break with the past memories of what he had done while drinking she would never change and risk letting him in. During one session I remember pushing her on this issue, and when she didn't know what to say she blurted out, "I can't control him. This is the problem. It has been that way since the day we got married."

Her husband answered her in a loud voice. "No!" he said. "That isn't the problem. The problem is that you are *trying* to control me. Why don't you stop trying to control me and work on yourself?"

As he continued in his healing process, they grew further and further apart. This demonstrates the importance of both parties being involved in the counseling. Unless both parties grow, the relationship becomes even more strained. And this one did . . . until one day the husband asked for a divorce. A divorce eventually happened because she was unwilling to break with the memories of the past. One party had become ready to be healed by Christ while the other party wouldn't break with the past. She wasn't ready. Even though she knew there was little change without the breaking, she was unwilling to let go of the past so that she could change the present.

Lord, change is hard . . .
  and becoming entirely ready is even harder.

It means I have to give up my false security,
  and I have to swallow my pride.

I have to be willing to break with my old habits
  so that Christ can heal me and
  help me to change my destructive lifestyle.

For I know now that there is little change without the breaking.

  Amen.

Little Healing without the Grieving[1]

"Taking her by the hand
he said to her . . .
'Little girl, I say to you, arise.'
And immediately the girl got up and walked. . . ."
Mark 5:41-42a

Human life unfolds in cycles and seasons. There are moments of exhilaration and times of routine, summers of certainty and autumns of doubt, springs of hope and winters of grief. We move through mountains and valleys, light and darkness, joy and sorrow.

Ten months before this writing, my foster brother Kermit died. As I look back, the week he died stands out as a week of changes. The Institute for Christian Living was in process of moving to its new location, and this was both exciting and fearful. All of us had been looking forward to a place that we could call ours, but it required acting on faith because it was going to be considerably more expensive than our previous location.

It was the day of the move. The office furniture was being moved from one building to the other, and I had no space in which to see people. As a result I happened to be with Kermit at the moment when he had a massive heart attack and slumped to the floor.

I did all of the proper things. I called "911" and within a couple of minutes the police came and started to resuscitate

---

[1]This chapter should be read with Step VII of the Twelve Steps for Christian Living: "We humbly ask Christ to transform all of our shortcomings."

him, and a few minutes later the ambulance from North Memorial Medical Center came. They worked on him for twenty minutes, doing all they could, but were unable to get a pulse. A decision was made to take him by ambulance to the Emergency Room and after about ten minutes he began to respond. They were finally able to get a pulse.

After being placed in the Coronary Care Unit at the hospital, he was put on a heart pump to help his breathing. This was about 3:00 PM. He remained on the pump for about fifteen hours. During this time his heart would beat irregularly and then his pulse would begin to weaken. This happened four or five times during this period. Each time the doctors and nurses would have to shock him in order to stabilize him and each time his blood pressure became weaker.

During that time, I will never forget those dear friends who were with me — taking me to the hospital, sitting with me in the Emergency Room, walking with me down the halls, and holding me as if to say, "It's okay to cry."

Death came at 5:20 AM the following day. My sense had been from the very beginning of the ordeal that Kermit would not survive, and if he did I was afraid that he might be a "vegetable." I told the doctor in the Emergency waiting room that I did not want any extraordinary methods used to keep him alive. I wanted him to have the right to die with dignity.

Kermit died Tuesday morning, we buried him Friday morning, and on Friday afternoon I left the city for the I.C.L.'s annual fall retreat. Some might wonder why I went or how I could go and be responsible for the retreat immediately after the funeral of my foster brother. Well, I couldn't have done it alone. There were at least four others that were there to help me, and most of all there was the comforting and upholding presence of MY LORD!

Jesus was certainly there with me. He was speaking to me all weekend. I was waking up at 2:00 AM unable to sleep, and instead of fighting it, I got up and began to write down my thoughts and feelings. My journaling became a very important part of my grieving process. Through my writing I was able to identify my pain, get it out, and let go of it . . . because there is LITTLE HEALING WITHOUT THE GRIEVING.

Through that weekend of solitude and dialoguing with my Lord, I again got in touch with my workaholism. The pressure of that week was more than typical for me, and yet, being the workaholic I was, I looked at it as "par for the course."

The theme of all our retreats is healing. We never approach healing in the same way twice and our aim is always to help people focus on the areas of their lives that need healing. Even though I was one of the leaders, this was MY weekend! I had time to hear what the Lord had to say to me — even all night long.

Most of my life I have been doing things for others, and I have usually done a lousy job of taking care of myself. Through my brother's death I got the message: "It could just as well have been you lying there on the floor with a massive heart attack!"

That weekend at the retreat I made four contracts. I vowed that I would do some things to nurture myself. First, I was going to visit some friends in Texas at Thanksgiving who I had not seen for ten years. I was also going to visit my real sisters in Florida at Christmas; the one sister I had not seen for twenty years. You see, I was always too busy, and helping others was too important to take time out even for family ties. Third, I was going to a retreat just for myself during Holy Week. I was always conducting retreats for everyone else, but I didn't take the time to go to one myself. Fourth, I was going to visit some family and friends in California.

Being the compulsive person that I am, I had all of these contracts completed in five and a half months. In addition, I began to exercise more, even jogging three times a week. My lifestyle was improving. Life was more meaningful because I was taking time to nurture myself, to love myself as God loves me, but not quite. My battle with my addiction to work was not over. I was back at work again. I slipped back into the old rut.

But there was a change. First of all, I recognized my work compulsion. Second, I didn't shame myself for it; I affirmed myself for the progress I had made and for the things I had been doing for myself. Third, I vowed to get back to taking better care of myself.

Overworking is still a problem for me. I can see it coming out even as I am writing this book. Less than two weeks have gone by since I began to write and I am already on the rough draft of the eighth chapter. I could rationalize and say that this is only because I am finally ready to write again, or that I am now an open vessel for the Lord to speak through me. Although both of these sound so holy and altruistic, maybe they do contain some truth. But I cannot and I will not deny my compulsivity and my workaholic behavior. It is still one of the "thorns in my flesh." Like the apostle Paul, "that which I would I don't do."

Yet, I would be remiss if I could not see the positive side of this character trait. The value of being obsessed with work is that hopefully now I can make good use of this obsession when "the spirit moves" and when I need to be productive. But I also need to put this obsession to rest so that I can slow down and take it easy once in awhile and allow myself to be nurtured. The Lord wants me to love myself! Otherwise, I will do a poor job of loving others.

Change can be traumatic and it can be ecstatic. Change can result from a crisis or from the constraining love of the Lord Christ. Either way, there is little healing without the grieving, but when the grieving is coupled with a responsive attitude of joy and gratitude, transformation becomes creative.

Change Requires Persistence

The parable of the widow and the unjust judge speaks to the issue of change. This parable points out that in order for Christ to help us to transform our lives, four things are required. First, we have to be courageously committed to change. Second, we have to actively pursue our changing and not wait for Christ to do it for us.

The account of the widow is an exciting story because we are left with the impression that persistence pays off and this can give us all hope. This woman in the parable had decided that she had the truth, and shows that she is not afraid of acting on that truth by confronting the judge. Many times our fear stops us. We know in our hearts that some of the changes we need to make are right, but we are afraid to act on them. We fear what others will say. We are afraid others won't like us. Sometimes it is easier to keep playing the game and not risk rejection than it is to change the behavior that enslaves us. Sometimes it seems easier to be in bondage than to risk experiencing freedom. Being the person that God created us to be requires persistence. This woman epitomized persistence. She was demanding. Her cause was no whim. Her need was real.

Traditionally, widows were to be pitied, but not this woman. Widows were considered outsiders, but she wouldn't be put out. Women without their husbands were valueless. They were even less important than a son of a concubine, but her worth was written all over her. Widows were stereotyped as helpless and defenseless, but she was her own defense. Nothing would get in her way. She would change the mind of that judge, and she did. Her persistence paid off. He got tired of her "beating" on him verbally and was willing to do almost anything to get her off his back.

The reason that Jesus tells this parable is to show the importance of prayer. "And he told them a parable, to the effect that they ought always to pray and not lose heart" (Luke 18:1). Jesus, however, does not say that this woman prayed to be treated justly. Yet, it is hard for me to believe that she got her courage and persistence only from her conviction that she was right. I believe that some of her feistiness came from her conviction, but also that she got some of it from God. I believe that she was humble enough to know that she couldn't change the judge by herself, even though she doesn't look like she needs any help from anyone. Perhaps the real source of her bravery comes from God who is RIGHTEOUSNESS for all of us.

It is true that there is no evidence that she prayed for God's help, but then there are some people who define prayer as ACTION. They know that God hears even the desires of our hearts, and certainly she was desirous of being treated justly and she showed it.

Finally, this widow didn't only have faith, but she acted on it. Her desire motivated her to act. She didn't merely sit and pray. She realized that if she was going to accomplish her task of justice, she was going to have to do it. She couldn't play the role of the helpless, defenseless widow. She would have to bring about justice through action.

Perhaps the chief sin of many is to wait to let God do it. This is not one of my sins, but mine is similar. Mine is the sin of letting others define who I am. This is the result of my people-pleasing and my lack of self-love, and I act this out by being a workaholic. I now realize that I need to use my compulsive persistence to stop the destructiveness of my workaholism. I need to use my compulsive persistence to have the courage to BECOME.

The widow was the kind of strong, courageous individual who I would like to think was becoming who she really was. She was unwilling to remain unimiportant, helpless and a non-person. She was not going to be a defenseless widow of whom others could take advantage. She found healing in her grieving. She found the courage to become.

His Son Had Just Died

The death of his son had occurred almost a year ago now. Yet, he was still immobilized by his depression. He was lethargic, downcast and hopeless. What is worse, his marriage was deteriorating. His wife insisted that he come in for counseling. She knew that he would lose his marriage if he didn't change his life. This was the second marriage for both of them. One failure was enough. Their self-esteem couldn't stand up to another loss, especially the loss of each other.

His son had been his whole life after his divorce. Even though his son was in poor health all of his life, the father felt driven to keep his son alive and functioning. He couldn't fail here, too. But in spite of all of his love and extraordinary efforts, his son died.

Even though he was married to his present wife at the time, she had become second in importance. He had given most of his time and energy to his son, and it hadn't paid off. He died! Had God failed him again? He felt like it, even though his knowledge told him different. His emptiness and loss were unbearable. His pain turned to anger, and his anger turned inward and had become depression. His grief, unresolved, was destroying him and his marriage.

I remember the first time he came to see me. We talked of his anger at God. We discussed his need to finish his grieving and prayed for his desire and ability to forgive so that he could let go of his pain and be healed. His healing continued that day. I say continued, because it had been on hold for months. As the months went by, he acted on his belief that Christ can heal; he committed himself to that process; he was persistent in pursuing it; and he humbly accepted Christ's help because he knew he could not be healed alone. He was being CREATIVELY TRANS-FORMED by the unconditional love of Christ and of his wife.

Life Takes Courage

The story of this man is not an uncommon one. Unfortunately there are far too many people who have lost their meaning for life—their life has lost its sweetness. This man had chosen to die inside rather than face another loss.

I have thought about him many times since he first came to see me. His story has stayed with me longer than I thought it would because I recognize myself in him.

Life takes a lot of courage. Life takes toughness and persistence. And when I think of this man who had chosen emotional and spiritual death, what is most clear is that I cannot let outside forces, events, or even people determine my life or my worth (as in the case of the widow), because then none of us is safe or saved (healed).

There are really only two ways to approach life: as an unimportant person, or as a person of worth. We need to decide either to be committed or to be irresponsible, to be persistent or to be permissive, to be prayerful or to be proud, so that we can be active and not left waiting.

There are many redeeming facts about courage, but there is one that is most significant. Courage grows with use. Courage must not be put on the shelf. If you don't use it, you lose it. You can't store courage away for a rainy day in hopes that it will be there for you. Most of us are stronger than we think. With Christ's help, we are able to change things we never though possible before.

It is hard to transform our shortcomings even with Christ's help. There aren't any guarantees. And sometimes we have practiced our bad habits so long that they seem like a friend, even though they are our worst enemies. Changing them seems too demanding and we opt for the emptiness instead of the joy of the abundant life.

Christ's transformation of our life requires that we dip into the depths of our being for the courage to act. And even though we have failed before and lost before, we know that the Lord, out of His everlasting love, wants us to become who we really are . . . even though this might mean that THERE IS LITTLE HEALING WITHOUT THE GRIEVING.

Lord, I want to become . . . Your precious child
who can laugh and cry,
who can play and work,
In order to know more fully Your life abundant.

Lord, I want to be transformed . . .
from boredom to joy;
from drudgery to gratitude.

Lord, thank You for the grieving . . .
For there is little healing without the grieving.
Amen

Little Soul
without the Waking[1]

"Formerly, when you did not know God,
you were in bondage to beings
that by nature are no gods;
but now that you have come to know God,
or rather to be known *by God,*
how can you turn back again to the
weak and beggarly elemental spirits,
whose slaves you want to be once more?"

Galatians 4:8-9

According to Paul, only the person who loves God is known by God. To be known by God is to be saved by His grace. But salvation is not only eternal or to be enjoyed in the life to come. Salvation is now! When Paul spoke of salvation in Philippians 2:12, he was referring to the here-and-now. The word salvation means healing and Paul is concerned that we "work out our own healing (salvation) with fear and trembling." This requires that we as Christians learn to know ourselves as God knows us and leave no room for a complacent attitude which says, "I know God." Step X is a continuation of Step IV, only Step X is to be done on a daily basis. "Spirituality reflects a lifelong response on the part of Christians to the grace of God, which changes us and allows us to grow."[2]

---

[1]This chapter should be read with Step X of the Twelve Steps for Christian Living: "We continue to take personal inventory and when we are wrong promptly admit it, and when we are right, thank God for His guidance."

[2]V. Bittner, "Study Guide," *You Can Help with Your Healing*, p. 20.

Without being "known by God" we will not know ourselves, and we will not come alive to the person we are. For there is LITTLE SOUL WITHOUT THE WAKING.

My Desert Experience

It was the Friday before Palm Sunday and I was about to fulfill one of the contracts that I had made back in November—to go to a retreat *just for* me. I had arrived at the airport in plenty of time to make the flight to Denver with the connecting flight to Albuquerque, New Mexico. My destination was Pecos, New Mexico, to attend a retreat at a Benedictine monastery on "Dreams and the Inner Journey."

I was excited! I was finally going to have some time away, some solitude for personal reflection. It was my time to think, to pray, to be silent and allow Christ to speak to me in any way He would.

Solitude had been something I knew I had always needed. Not that one has to go to New Mexico to be alone, but sometimes we have to leave our familiar environment to make solitude happen. I think that one of the reasons I had avoided my own retreat was that I was using my workaholism to run from some of the real questions of life, and I didn't want to run any more. My work had only superficially filled up my life. When the work was finished I was always left with a deeper sense of isolation. I had avoided the real issue—the need for an intimate friendship where I could share all of myself.

Solitude provides the time and space to discover the shape and direction of our spiritual journey. In solitude we have the chance to allow Christ to transform our isolation into a deeper sensitivity to our own life, to our relationship with God and with our neighbor. But all of these high expectations suddenly were on hold. It was snowing and the Denver airport was closed down except for one runway.

After a two and a half hour delay, my plane finally took off. During that time I began to wonder if the Lord was telling me that I should have stayed home and remained addicted to my work. I knew that these thoughts were only the devil's trying to talk me out of doing something for my own spiritual growth.

The flight to Denver was good, but I just missed my connecting flight to Albuquerque. A few years ago I would have felt like pulling out my hair if something like this happened. My impulsive nature would have caused me to start pacing the floor and bugging the people at the desk, but now I was taking it as it came. Six hours later I was finally able to get on a plane out of Denver. After being bumped off several waiting lists on two different airlines, I was one of ten out of forty-five stand-by passengers to get on the last plane that night for Albuquerque.

I arrived in Albuquerque at 11:00 PM and decided to rent a car. Several times during the past seven and a half hours I had wondered what the Lord was trying to say to me. Trusting my belief that I needed to go to this retreat for myself, I started driving toward Pecos.

After driving about 50 miles toward the mountains, it began to snow. Again I wondered if this was really what the Lord wanted me to do. I had already missed the whole first evening of the retreat and most people would have waited until morning to go to a place they had never been to before.

Eventually about twenty miles later, hardly able to see because I was driving in a blizzard, I saw the sign. As I drove off the freeway I was filled with mixed feelings. The road appeared to be gravel and I had visions of spending the night in the ditch.

It was almost 1:00 AM and I had driven five miles on this road. I had no idea of the location of the monastery. In the distance I could see a light. I decided to stop and see if they could tell me the location of the moastery. The light was coming from a trailer house at the end of a long driveway. I knocked on the door and was greeted by a slightly inebriated man who seemed a little confused, but said it was about three miles down the road.

He was right, but now that I was there, how would I get in, and where was I to sleep? Within twenty minutes I found a key with my name on it and proceeded to the room. I unlocked the door, turned on the light, and a half naked man jumped up from one of the beds with his arms raised high in the air and shouted, "Don't shoot! Don't shoot!" Again, I wondered if this was really what the Lord wanted me to do. I was able to find another bed that was empty and slept a short but thankful night.

During my time alone that week we were led on a guided imagery in which we spoke with each of our parents. We were told that we could say anything we wanted to either of our parents. I had nothing to say to my father because I had put a closure on that relationship. But as I was talking to my mother I got in touch with my need to have her hold me and tell me she loved me. Apparently, her untimely death when I was seven resulted in my not feeling loved and cherished as a child.

I realized that my "wounded child" was still in need of healing. Perhaps this was one of the reasons that intimacy and closeness had been so frightening for me in the past. Much of that week was spent in prayer and meditation that the Lord would continue healing my wounded "boy" so that he would stop getting in the way of my adult relationships.

That Holy Week was truly a spiritual time for me. That time alone confirmed once again for me that I *do* matter. I felt like crying out as loud as I could: "I am! I exist! I do make a difference!" But to cry this is not only to assert that "I am," but it is also to ask the question, "How am I to be who I am? What difference DO I make?" This experience made me realize again that I am not yet who I am to become. That time alone was my Passover, and out of that Pecos desert experience I learned to know more of my hidden self because I allowed myself to be known by God. For there is LITTLE SOUL WITHOUT THE WAKING.

Suggestions for an Inventory

Paul challenges us to continue to work daily on our spiritual life. He is concerned that we not go back to being ungrateful beggars whose lives are empty and without meaning. He wants us to be free to become all that God created us to be. This means that we are to keep working on being known by God, knowing ourselves so that we can work on the areas in which we need to grow.

Taking an inventory of our daily performance is a necessary part of working on continuing to have Christ transform our lives. The way this can be done creatively is by placing ourselves in the loving presence of God. Ignatius of Loyola has suggested five simple steps to follow. This is best done at night and will only take five to ten minutes.

The first step is *Thanksgiving*. For a short period of time, review the day and recall all of the gifts that God has given you, and directly thank Him for these gifts.

The second step is *Illumination*. Here we are to ask the Holy Spirit to help us see ourselves as we are, both sons and daughters of a loving Father. In addition, we are to look at ourselves as being in need of healing.

The third step is *Assessment*. Here we are to use Jesus as the norm and take an inventory of the day. See what thoughts, words or actions were least praiseworthy and look at how you might improve what you do tomorrow. Also, look at the behavior that was positive and thank God for His help.

The fourth step is *Forgiveness*. Like the Prodigal son, we need forgiveness. We must believe that there is forgiveness through Christ and see our need to accept it.

The fifth step is to ask God the Father, Son and Holy Spirit to be with you and help you do better tomorrow.

In addition to this inventory, I find it helpful to write in a journal the first thing in the morning. This accomplishes two things for me: it records my dreams so that I do not forget them, and it allows myself to be known by God, so that I can get in touch with myself. Then, depending on whether I am up or down, I can reach out to God accordingly and He can help me, either to give me strength for the day or for me to respond to Him in joyful gratitude. For there is little soul without the waking, and solitude is a necessary part of the waking.

Loving Is Knowing

If we are to grow in loving ourselves, we need to continue to know ourselves, and this is why Step X is so important. One of the results of my being addicted to work has been that I haven't taken the time to look at my life. As I have said before, perhaps the reason for my "busy-ness" was simply because I couldn't bear to turn inward and quietly look at myself.

You see, each of us has a part of us that we don't like. The part we don't like is the part that often doesn't perform right and most always falls on its face. And then the rageful person within us becomes self-condemning. It is this part of us that wants revenge and is bent on hatred even when there seems to be no reason for it. Perhaps this is the reason we all avoid looking at our daily performance.

On the other hand, there is the genuine caring side of all of us which enjoys giving love and being warm and nurturing. It is this part of us that is not only genuinely interested in others, but also is interested in itself. It is the spirit of Christ within, and it is this spirit that many of us don't tap or respond to on a regular basis. This spirit can most naturally be seen in the love of a mother for her child, a lover for the beloved, and a friend for a friend.

Yet, to truly love, we need to look at all of ourselves on a *regular* basis. We need to look at both sides of us. This is the only way we can monitor our destructive side and call forth our creative side. It is also the only way we can keep the growing process going, and if we are not progressing we are retreating, probably, as Paul says, "to the weak and beggarly elemental spirits, whose slaves you want to be once more."

In order to grow in our self awareness, we must come before God daily, in our morning time of meditation, prayer, and journaling, as well as during our evening time when we inventory our day. When we do this we must bring all of ourselves and all of our behavior before God. It is only in being known by God that we can know His love and therefore love ourselves.

Letting God know us and getting to know God is very difficult to do unless we are willing to take time for silence and solitude.

Allowing time alone makes it possible to journal, listen to our dreams, our fantasies, and daydreams, and look at our loves and hates. Unless we take time for solitude, I don't believe that we can really appreciate the time we spend with the important other(s) in our lives. Such times of solitude can become the occasions when we discover a deeper sense of communion with those whom we love.

Perhaps the reason for taking such time for solitude is that when we discover our uniqueness more clearly, we are then better able to develop and grow in our interdependent relationships. Solitude, I believe, can energize us, because we have experienced the creative love of Christ. Solitude is not to be considered a time to escape from people and the burdens of life, but rather it is a time to discover the ways in which we are one with God and others.

Often though we are not able to bear all of our self knowledge alone, nor are we able to assimilate it. We need another soul-mate besides Jesus. We need a trusted friend with whom we can share all of whom we are. Many times we need to do such sharing on a daily basis. This person or persons can help us be more objective with ourselves. In addition, they can encourage, challenge and support us in our spiritual quest to be more fully the person that God created us to be. We need a special friend or friends who can feed our spirit and even our senses. We need friends that can help us to stretch different sides of ourselves, and in order to do such stretching we need to dialogue with some other person besides God.

I know that there are a lot of people who believe in one best friend, and hopefully this best friend is both our friend and lover. Even though I tend to agree with this, I am coming to believe that most people need more than one special person. No one person can meet all of our emotional needs because no one is perfect. Maybe we need four or five friends to help us to look at ourselves and help us to be more ourselves. Obviously our time will dictate how many and how often these relationships will occur. Yet, these friends are important because without them we can't see ourselves as we are, or grow to be what we were intended to be.

I believe that women are recognizing the value of this and perhaps are better able to share on an emotional level. However, it seems that men have more difficulty with such sharing. Too often men see other people as things to be conquered or held off. Many men have allies and they also have enemies, but few of them really have friends, and that is why so many marriages are not doing very well. By this I am not saying that it is all the man's problem, but I am saying that men usually have more difficulty sharing all of themselves than women do.

Unfortunately, we are a success-oriented society, so a lot of men put their energy into getting ahead and not into time alone or time with trusted friends. And unfortunately, many men and women think of fulfillment as something to be found in money and things, and don't learn until it is too late that the only wealth that really counts is having at least two soulmates — God and a trusted friend(s).

Coming to be known by God on a daily basis involves solitude as well as time with a trusted friend. Daily we need to be known by God so that we can more fully know ourselves. Without this regular walk with ourselves and God, life will become static. Daily experiencing the love of God and others makes life more dynamic and creative. Without such daily experiences transformation would not be continuous, and unless transformation occurs daily, it is not really transformation. Transformation is a process, not an event.

Lord, solitude can be lonely and frightening...
  and yet loneliness and being alone are two different things.
Solitude helps us to take time to be known by God...
  so that we can know ourselves.
Solitude gives us space to know ourselves as God knows us...
  so that our growth can pro-gress and not re-gress.
In solitude there is the energy we need to discover
    a deeper sense of communion...
  with those we love and those who love us...
For THERE IS LITTLE SOUL WITHOUT THE WAKING.
    Amen

Part III
Others

In this final section, we see the importance of loving others and how necessary this is for creative transformation. Unless we become willing to make amends, be reconciled with the important people in our life, and share the love of Christ's friendship with others, we will not know the joy of loving others. Without that LOVE experience with others, we will not really know creative transformation. Transformation only becomes creative when Christ's love is experienced on a human level. Without this personal love experience, transformation will not continue to grow and have any lasting effect. For loving and being loved on a human level is what makes transformation creative, and thereby lasting.

"Don't hide your light!
Let it shine for all;
let your good deeds glow
for all to see,
so that they will praise
your heavenly Father."
Matthew 5:15-16, *The Living Bible*

Little Love
without Receiving[1]

*"But love your enemies, and do good,
and lend, expecting nothing in return;
and your reward will be great;
and you will be sons/daughters of the most high;
for he is kind to the ungrateful and selfish.
Be merciful even as your father is merciful."*
Luke 6:35-36

There are some who would define love as just being in the presence of another and acting love out in any way that appeals to them. Surely this explains why there have been some terrible things done in the name of love.

There are others who would see love as that which moves us toward another because we see value and worth in that person. This love is called "eros," and is usually done out of a selfish motivation because of what we might be able to receive for ourselves. This, too, is not always a very kind act, and yet can be loving in nature because it is giving, even though such love is done with the anticipation of getting love in return.

The noblest form of love is reaching out to another in order to give, not to get. This is usually called "agape" love. It is not being loving because the other person is lovable. It is loving another in spite of who they are. It is the love that does not seek to be filled up, but to fill the other. It is a love that desires to nurture and replenish without any expectations for the self.

[1]This chapter should be read with Step VIII of the Twelve Steps for Christian Living: "We make a list of all persons we have harmed and become willing to make amends to them all."

At face value this kind of love seems almost divine, not human. It seems unattainable. Perhaps, in its purest form it is unattainable. Yet, this is the kind of love we are to strive for as Christians.

But how can "agape" love happen? How can we be motivated to love others without any reward—except the joy of loving? The New Testament tells us that the origin of this love is God. We can love only because we have been loved by God.[1] And because we have been given His love, we are able to love ourselves.[2]

But why did God love us? He wanted to share, to nurture and to save us because we were lacking and couldn't experience such love by ourselves.[3] He loved us because He wanted to give, not to get. And because we have been loved, we can love not only ourselves, but others as well, for there is LITTLE LOVE WITHOUT RECEIVING!

Forgiveness Is "Becoming Willing"

There have been times in my life, and maybe yours, when things have not been the way I have wanted them to be. There have been times when all of us have said, "As a child of God, I deserve a richer and fuller life. Why isn't life more meaningful?" Some of us, like myself, have tried to make ourselves be something other than what God intended us to be. Sometimes that is okay and for the good of all. But most often such self direction leads to discontent, resentment, and the hurting of others as well as ourselves.

Perhaps the reason for making ourselves something other than what God intended us to be is because many people have not found a creative task to which to give themselves. There is nothing more creative for the lover or the beloved than to give love. I believe that we as human beings have three basic needs: to love God, to feel a sense of worth (self love), and to love and be loved. Not only are these needs the emphasis of this book, but they are also what

---

[1] This is covered in Part I.
[2] This was covered in Part II.
[3] Step I: "We admit our need for God's gift of salvation, that we are powerless over certain areas of our lives and that our lives are at times sinful and unmanageable."

give meaning to life and are the essence of the "Twelve Steps for Christian Living.[1]

I used to think that being a people pleaser was what Christianity was all about. After all, wasn't I giving? Wasn't I loving my enemies? Yes, I was, but I was loving for the wrong reasons. I was expecting a payoff. I was hoping to be loved. And when the rewards were not forthcoming I felt abused and used and became resentful and withdrawn. I would remain that way until I would either guilt myself, be guilted by someone else, or just get tired of being there. Then I would continue on another binge of pleasing others. I played out this destructive behavior over and over again for three-fourths of my life without any transforming or creative results. The only result was loneliness.

After living most of my life I have experienced that loneliness is a choice, just as love is a choice. And IF YOU DON'T RUN AFTER LONELINESS YOU WON'T CATCH IT. On the other hand, if you choose to give love, you will receive it. Love is not only pleasing others; love is sometimes confronting others and caring enough to help them toward being the creative persons for which God made them.

There is a difference between aloneness and loneliness. Loneliness is something we do to ourselves. Those who choose loneliness take it with them everywhere they go. I am convinced that most of my loneliness has resulted from the feelings of hurt and anger in my attempt to be loved and accepted by pleasing others. Usually these lonely feelings have lasted as long as I have refused to "become willing to make amends"[2] to acquire forgiving attitudes. To become willing to make amends requires an attitude of forgiveness. Not only does Step VIII require forgiveness, but working this step is the BEGINNING OF FRIEND-SHIP. Not only am I unable to love without God's love, but I won't experience love without giving it. So there is LITTLE LOVE WITHOUT RECEIVING the love from God, and there

---

[1]See the "Twelve Steps for Christian Living" listed on page 123.
[2]Taken from the words of Step VIII of the Twelve Steps for Christian Living: "We make a list of all persons we have harmed and become willing to make amends to them all."

is little love without then returning the love which has been given.

Loving the Enemy Is "Becoming Willing"

Unless we are able to love our enemies, it may be very difficult to make amends to those we have harmed. The reason I say this is that our enemies have been some of the people we have harmed because our anger has come out destructively. On the other hand, many times the people we have hurt the most are those who are closest to us. Perhaps this is because we have taken their love for granted. We assume that they will love us no matter what we do. Consequently, they become our enemy, either consciously or unconsciously, either by our seeing them this way or by their actually being an enemy in our life.

Often I see this when I am attempting to do marriage counseling with a couple. Instead of being lovers and friends, they appear to be enemies. They are resentful, hypercritical, and unwilling to admit their wrongs. They are reluctant to make amends because they refuse to love the enemy they see in the other person. And many times that enemy is really the enemy within themselves. Usually the part we dislike most in others is the part of ourselves that we unconsciously reject.

Jesus makes it very clear that real spiritual maturity begins when we begin to love our enemy, not only in others but in ourselves as well. Until we get to the point of being able to reach out to those who mistreat us and who despitefully use us, we will not be WILLING to make amends with others and ourselves.

Not only did Jesus teach this, but He lived it. We are not only to love those who love us, but we are to love the enemy as well. "If you love those who love you, what credit is it to you? For even sinners love those who love them" (Luke 6:33).

This challenge from Jesus is both inspiring and humbling. To believe that it is possible to love our enemies is to know that each of us possesses a touch of the divine. Yet, to know that we are expected to love our enemies in order to be mature Christians makes us realize how inadequate we are.

But what does it mean to love our enemies? I used to believe and attempt to live out the philosophy that loving did not include liking. In other words, I could love a person, but I didn't have to like them. Recently I have been struck by the insight that it is pretty hard to love someone in Christian love without liking them. Loving without liking is not loving at all.

Have you ever been loved by someone who didn't like you? I haven't! Oh, they may have gone through the motions of loving me. But real love carries with it a sense of caring in which we are able to find at least something appealing in the other person.

Some of you may be thinking to yourselves as you are making a list of those to whom you need to make amends, "I suppose if I look hard enough and long enough I might, just might be able to find something I can like." That is a rather humorous thought isn't it? Especially when we realize that some people are having the same problem with us.

To find something that we can like in our enemies does not mean that we approve of everything these people are doing. Some of the things they are doing may be causing a great deal of harm and hurt and are irresponsible in nature. But as Christians, we can still find some quality we can like, if we are not too judgmental, in order to love them.

Jesus' challenge to us to love our enemies is a part of His great commandment to "love your neighbor as you love yourself." What does this mean? How do we actually love ourselves? It is not being plagued with the compulsion of looking at ourselves in a mirror and wallowing in our own virtues. This is narcissism and pure selfishness.

To love ourselves is to want for ourselves the best that life can give and to be assertive enough to pursue it. This, however, does not mean that we have a license to walk on others to achieve such love. It does mean that we possess a humble recognition of the real values of life: to love God, ourself, and others. Then loving ourselves means to achieve for ourselves the ultimate enrichment which God can give, and this is the abundant life. Loving our neighbor and even our enemy means that we would want all that is best for them as well as for ourselves in life. We would want their life to be transformed by the love of Christ so that they could experience the abundant life.

Perhaps one of the most effective ways of loving one's enemies and wanting what is best for them is to pray for them. Jesus tells us that we are to "pray for those who persecute you" (Matthew 5:44). I find that praying for those I dislike and the people that dislike me is useful in changing my attitudes. When I am praying for these people, I image them in my mind and I see Christ with them, loving them and caring for them.

If, in our praying, we can ask God's care and protection for these people, it helps prevent us from saying or doing anything unkind to them. Any negative action would be at odds with what we are asking our Lord to do and would discourage our actions from being loving. I am convinced that it is very possible for us to love people that we would like to hate. Love is a choice just as resentment is a choice. We can harbor anger and nurse it until it will consume us, or we can decide to let go of it.

I remember counseling a man some time ago who was almost always angry at his wife for something. In fact, we used to joke about it. Laughing at his useless anger was in itself a helpful process. I would often ask him, "How long do you want to stay angry at her this time? An hour? A day? A week? Or would you rather be angry for six months or a year?" He would begin laughing because he realized how ridiculous it was for him to nurse his resentment.

However, the process that was most helpful for him was praying for his wife, especially when he was angry. It was through prayer that he began to realize that anger was his security. In order to feel strong and confident with her, he would have to get a "mad on." Otherwise, he felt he would have trouble holding his own with her, and she would dominate him. There are still so many people who feel that the only way not to be controlled is to be the dominant one.

Thirty years ago, when I was having trouble in my walk with the Lord, I used to think that prayer was a useless exercise. I know now that it isn't. In fact, the studies being made in parapsychology show that we have non-sensory ways of reaching out to other people. Therefore, space and time cannot block our influence on others. If we come to the Lord and are willing to pray in an earnest and sincere way, our caring often gets through to the other person. Unfortunately, our hatred can also get through to another person. We need to realize that there is more power in prayer than we could know. It is possible to communicate our concern and love if we have the imagination and desire to pray. For there is little love without receiving, and maybe love will not be received without our yearning to have others, especially our enemies, make love a part of their life so that they can experience it.

How to Become Willing

The first step in becoming willing to make amends is to realize that all of us fall short when it comes to loving our enemies. Not only do we dislike, avoid, and punish our enemies, but we don't even walk the extra mile for those enemies who are close to us. Often the enemy is right within our own family or within ourselves. If we do any reflecting at all on our behavior, most of us are shocked at how little love we have in our lives. Also, we are painfully aware of how little of the things we do are motivated by love.

Second, we need to accept that being willing means that we stop avoiding those to whom we need to make amends, not only physically but mentally as well. In order to become ready to make amends, we have to mentally picture those we have hurt and get to the place where we are desirous of facing them. Perhaps the most hostile act is to ignore people. Yet, there are times when this is the only action that will stop some people from using us. But we need to remember that we are social beings and being out of touch with the important people in our lives has caused some to actually wither and die. In many cultures, being removed from a group was considered to be a punishment equal to that of death.

Third, making amends and loving our enemies may involve suffering. We need to be prepared for suffering and not approach it with a naivete that all people we have hurt will welcome us with open arms. Even Jesus, who was perfect, was persecuted when He sought to love people. The Pharisees were threatened by Him because He brought with Him a spirituality that they were unwilling to try. It was too nebulous, it required too much self-responsibility, and its freedom was too overwhelming.

What is even more threatening than suffering might be our spiritual maturity. The fact that we are willing to make amends may add to the guilt and anxiety of those to whom we make amends. When this is the case, the chasm between the enemy and ourselves may become greater. Our enemies may feel even more angry at us because of their own unwillingness to accept our apology and forgive us. Consequently they may respond by inflicting even more enmity upon us, and what we thought was going to be healing might even be more painful.

Finally, we must realize that making amends means that we will be facing people who probably do not like us. So not only will we have to encounter people we have not liked, but those who probably still don't like us. We may even have to deal with people who pride themselves in the fact that they have well-rooted resentments within them that they have had for years. It is one thing to have resentments (and we all have them), and it is another thing to feel proud about them.

Therefore, to become willing to make amends requires the following: We must admit to falling short of Christ's expectation that we love our enemies; we must stop avoiding thinking about these people and start facing them; we must accept that making amends may involve suffering; and we must understand that they will probably not like us.

Considering all of these facets might cause us to continue to want to avoid making amends. Yet, to do this without looking at all of the ramifications would not be doing what is necessary to really be prepared to become willing. Becoming willing is being prepared even to love our enemies. Becoming willing is desiring to love enough to be willing to swallow our false pride and to apologize for the wrongs we have done to others without any expectations. This is the highest form of love. This is "agape" love. It is only in being willing to love in this way that we will experience the true joy of loving. For THERE IS LITTLE LOVING WITHOUT RECEIVING, even though agape love receives by experiencing the joy of giving love and expects nothing in return.

Lord, loving...What is it?
  Is it just being and acting out?
  Is it loving those who love us?
  Is it loving those who we feel attracted toward?
  Or is it a desire to give?

So often, Lord, my loving is so shallow...
  Because it is only giving to GET!

Help me, Lord, to love even my enemies
  So that I become ready to make amends with those I've hurt.

Teach me, Lord, that this is really the only way to receive...
  the joy of loving and being loved.

For there is little love without receiving...
  even the joy of giving love without any expections.

  Amen

Little Receiving without the Bringing[1]

"A man once gave a great banquet, and invited many;
and at the time for the banquet he sent his servant to
those who had been invited, 'Come, for all is now ready.'
But they all alike began to make excuses.
The first said to him, 'I bought a field and I must go out
and see it; I pray you, have me excused...
Then the householder in anger said to his servant,
'Go out quickly to the streets and lanes of the city,
and bring in the poor and maimed and blind and lame..
For I tell you, none of those men/women who were invited
shall taste my banquet.'"

Luke 14:16-24

I am sure that Jesus was telling
this parable because He wanted Christians to know that to follow Him and to really live the mature Christian life meant that
we would have to stop giving ourselves excuses for the things
we need to do that would bring about spiritual growth.

There are many people who beg off in life. There are a lot of
ways to avoid doing what might be painful or what might require
us to swallow our pride. All of us have been involved in our share
of procrastination. Even more interesting, many of us at times believe that we have done everything humanly possible to be reconciled, and we are so convinced of this that we even fool ourselves.

---

[1]"This chapter should be read with Step IX of the Twelve Steps for Christian Living: "We make
direct amends to such persons wherever possible, except when to do so would injure them or
others.

We so often procrastinate in relationships with the important others in our life. We need to remember this when we are disappointed in our friendships or when we disappoint others. Some people give up early and others later in their commitments, and few people keep on giving no matter how difficult or painful the experience may be.

I wish I could say that all of the people we love will love us back, or that all of our needs and the needs of those closest to us will always be the same. But life isn't that way. We are all unique and have different needs. Some of the things we have wanted, or that others have wanted from us, were not available and if they were, they may not have been given.

This lack of getting what we have felt we have needed often results in our hurting and being hurt. When this happens we must admit to our part of the problem and be willing to do all we can to mend the situation. Otherwise, we will be alienated, separated, or isolated. We will miss the dynamic healing GIFT of life which is LOVE.

The reality is that we are all essentially alone, and sometimes the people we love will let us in or will be there for us. Other times we can't be there for each other, no matter how hard we all try. Usually this results in hurt, anger and estrangement. When we are not there for our friends or they are not there for us, we feel ripped off. We even begin to question the value of the relationship. To avoid some of this hurt and separation, we need to remember that we usually don't get from friends what we give them; we only get what they can give. People, you and I, are only able to give what we *have* to give. If we are not getting what we need or if we are not allowed to give what we have to give, we might have to go some place else.

Yet, we must remember that no one person can meet all of our needs. Also, I am convinced that people are usually only able to be friends in certain places in our lives. There are people we would like to socialize with, but we wouldn't risk crying with them. We need to learn which is which, and remember that we don't need a lot of people to jog with if what we desire is a soul mate with whom we can share our hidden self. Therefore, there will be times when we will hurt others and be hurt by others. When this happens we need to be sensitive enough and courageous enough to mend the relationship.

Making "direct amends to" the people that we have harmed "will greatly benefit our life, and will help us to know the joy of forgiveness."[1] Often the only way this can be accomplished is if we willingly go personally to those with whom we feel estranged and do all that we can with the help of Christ to be reconciled. Hopefully, those to whom we go will be open and accept our desire for reconciliation. For there is LITTLE RECEIVING WITHOUT THE BRINGING, and the greatest gift is loving enough to be willing to make direct amends.

Christ's Invitation

Spiritual growth and Christian maturity is a process of removing the layers that cover the hidden self so that we will be able to see God's light more clearly (Psalm 36:9). The several excuses in the parable of the banquet seem innocent enough in themselves. Certainly, we need what agriculture can produce such as food and clothing. In addition, we need to have homes that will provide shelter and love. But all of these things are empty without a relationship to God. God must come first in our life and we must not let anything get in the way of doing His will. Many times doing God's will may involve our relationship with others, either our lack of it or loving enough to do what is necessary for mending it. Our friendship with others and also our friendship with God requires work. We cannot work on one without working on the other. The two go together.

The three excuses picture what society would consider important. In addition, they point out the problem which we all have at times of avoiding those things which are difficult to do and which we really know are necessary for growth and transformation. In this parable, Jesus is telling us that we have all been invited to His banquet. It is a heavenly banquet because it promises to bring us the abundant life. Significantly, this parable

---

[1]V. Bittner, "Study Guide," *You Can Help with Your Healing*, p. 19.

precedes His definition of what it means to be a disciple. I am sure its place is not coincidental, because being a disciple means that He must be first in our lives, and that we are committed to doing His will, especially to mend broken relationships.

The way the people refuse the invitation is significant. "I pray you, have me excused." They are so polite and so phony! They seem nearly moved to tears because they cannot attend. Matthew's version (22:1-10) says that they "made light of" the banquet.

How often do we think *our* way is better? How often do we think we can do it ourselves without the Lord's help? And how often do we want to tell Him what is necessary to transform our lives? At times we are so locked into our own selfish needs and our desires to be comfortable that we avoid doing the things that stretch us and transform us so that we can experience the joy which the Lord has in store for us.

I have sometimes wondered why God put Himself at such a disadvantage. He hardly has a chance to transform us with our desire for wealth, power, and sex, let alone our fear of intimacy and our doing what feels good. We often pass up the "pearl of great price" for rose colored glasses, and we miss the dynamic that makes life creative—reconciling relationships.

Next, the drama mounts. When the invited guests refuse the invitation, the king does a strange thing. He doesn't cancel the party. Instead, he invites the have-nots. The "nice people" are replaced by the poor and the blind, the murderers and the harlots, the godless and the alien, even though these people have been broken by cruelty and their own sin.

Unless we who call ourselves Christians are willing to allow the Lord to transform our lives, we will not know a life of joy and gratitude. We will be worse off than those who are outside the church. What is necessary is that we are open to His invitation. It doesn't matter who we are, whether we are the chosen or the lost. His response is the same. He loves us unconditionally. All He requires is that we love Him in return and love our neighbor as ourselves—even to be willing to make direct amends. For just as there is no reconciliation without amends, there is little receiving without the bringing.

He Couldn't Swallow His Pride

If we are willing to respond to the invitation of Christ to experience the abundant life we will know the joy of meaningful relationships. Making direct amends to the important others in our life is essential if we expect any kind of friendship to blossom. Fulfilling the requirements of the ninth step enables us to more truly love our neighbor.

Now there may be some who would wonder how any good could come from making amends, especially if making amends involves confessing our sins to the important people in our life. Yet, unless we are willing to do this we cannot have any kind of honest or intimate relationships.

I remember the man who came to me some time ago. He was going through what he called a mid-life crisis. He was forty years old and his wife was about the same age. At the time he was separated from his wife, and his son was with his wife. His problem was that he had never given himself the chance to *be* himself. His parents were very controlling. He learned as a child that the way to get along was to do what they wanted, but he resented every minute of it. He went from one dependent re-lationship to another. His wife was almost a carbon copy of his parents, and when she wasn't, he forced her into that position. Even when she tried to be his wife he saw her as a parent and he became the rebellious child. As time went on in their twenty year marriage, he became more and more isolated and withdrawn. The only needs that he expected her to meet were sexual. He was starved for emotional closeness even though he was not consciously aware of it. And unknowingly he found emotional closeness at work.

So many times people will say to me that they don't understand how an extra-marital relationship happened. My comment to them is, "You must have been looking for one or you wouldn't have found one." Their reaction is usually a combination of amazement and anger. They are appalled that I should come to such a conclusion. Then I explain to them that it was probably unconscious since only about thirty to seventy percent of what we do is conscious. This is the reason why it is so important to become more aware of our hidden self by working the fourth and the tenth steps.[1] I am convinced that most of the evil in this world is caused by people who are not conscious of their behavior.

This friendship outside the marriage continued until it developed into a physical relationship. It was then that he decided to move out of the house. It was a hard decision and one that he did not want to make. But how could he tell his wife what he had done? She would be furious. His pride had gotten in the way. Keeping his image of being the "good guy" was more important than risking making amends with his with his wife, resolving his dependency needs of the past, admitting that he had put her into the role of the parent, and working on developing an emotionally intimate relationship with his wife. His lack of humility wouldn't allow him to enjoy what he had built with his wife for twenty years, and his guilt wouldn't allow him to stay in the marriage. All he would have to do was tell his wife what had happened. In fact, she suspected it anyway. You can't live with a person for twenty years and not know them, at least somewhat. Women seem to have the innate gift of being intuitive, even though they may have no visible proof.

He went through with the divorce, and did eventually remarry. Now he is doing the same thing he did in his first marriage. His second wife has again been set up as the parent and he is again the rebellious child. So many people think that divorce is the solution. Often divorce does not solve the problems of the marriage, it only perpetuates the problems unless each person is willing to work on their own individual lives.

Having a good marriage takes a lot of hard work. Each person has to be willing to give and each has to be big enough to swallow

---

[1] See Chapters V and IX.

their pride, admit their part of the problem, and trust the Holy Spirit that through the process of making amends reconciliation will take place. For there is little receiving the gift of love without the bringing.

But what happens if you go to that important person and they reject you and condemn you and refuse to forgive you? This is *their* problem then, unless you have used poor judgment in how you told them, or poor judgment as to whether you should have told them at all. As the step says, we are to "make direct amends... except when to do so would injure them or others."

There are times when confessing our wrong would do more damage than withholding it. For example, you wouldn't tell your ninety-five year old mother who is senile that you have hated her most of your life and that now you want to confess this so that you can let go of it and be able to forgive her. Even though this example is somewhat exaggerated, it does illustrate the point. Obviously, your mother would not understand and it would be too hurtful for her to handle considering her current condition.

However, if someone fails to forgive when we attempt to make amends, this then becomes their sin. This does not mean that we shouldn't expect them to feel hurt, be angry, and even have difficulty accepting us and being reconciled. Yet, if they continue to condemn us and refuse to forgive us because they are not willing to see their part of the problem, there is not much we can do. We can, of course, give them some time and even space if this is what they need. But resolving these feelings becomes their problem, especially if they are suffering from self-righteousness.

The Key Is Love

The key to making direct amends is LOVE. Whatever else mending relationships may ask of us, reconciliation requires love. To love those important people in our lives enough to be willing to make direct amends means that we do three things: share ourselves, affirm the other person, and ask for guidance from the Holy Spirit to know when we should refrain from making direct amends.

There is a lot to be said for accepting the reality that all people, including ourselves, have limitations.[1] Once we understand this, then we realize that no love relationship can exist without pain. When we realize this we can be more content and more easily pleased with life, and we stop being judgmental of others.

When we truly love, we are open to receiving both sides of a person as well as sharing both sides of ourselves: the broken and the resentful, the thoughtful and the gifted. When we truly love, we are understanding and willing to risk that we *will* be understood, and when this happens, the good in both of us is called forth. This is the only way to make amends—to share ourselves. Self-disclosure is the only gift that lasts because this is the way we give ourselves. Flowers, jewelry and furs are only tokens of the real thing. If we haven't given our true and authentic self, we haven't given anything. There will be little mending of relationships and little emotional and spiritual closeness unless we are willing to share all of ourselves. Then when love happens, we cherish the experience, even if this love is only for a few minutes or for a week. We see this love as a gift and we are grateful for the one who has given it to us. Instead of being angry because there wasn't any love, we praise God for the one who brought love. We remember that there is little receiving without the bringing.

Making amends is also one of the effective ways of affirming the people we love. To apologize for the hurt we have caused is telling another that we care enough about them that we are willing to humble ourselves in their presence.

If we are to love the important people in our life, we need to let them know how much we appreciate them for the unique persons they are. In our relationships with others we are always in a position to build up or tear down. If we are loved we possess a great deal of power over another person. This is why mending relationships is so important. Mending is our way of contributing either positively or negatively. And if we are willing to

---

[1]See Chapter I, Step I.

make amends by "speaking the truth in love,"[1] we will confirm the other person's worth and value.

Finally, knowing when it is appropriate to make direct amends is sometimes difficult. The key again is LOVE. However, it also takes a prayerful attitude that is willing to be open to God's will, and then to have the courage to act on this will. Whatever we believe to be God's will, to withhold or to share it in honest love, we need to trust the Holy Spirit that the process will work. We need to believe that "in everything God works for good with those who love him, who are called according to his purpose..."[2] even when there is no reconciliation.

We also need to remember that we can only do our part. When we have done what we feel the Lord wants us to do, we need to trust what we have done and not second-guess ourselves. We cannot control the other person, take total responsibility for what happens, or expect that we will perform perfectly. When we have done our best, we need to "let go" and put the situation in God's hands. Maybe the person we are making amends with won't want to be reconciled immediately. Reconciliation might take years or even a death to come about.

Some time ago I was finally reconciled with a family member when a death occurred. The separation had been going on for over two years. It often takes such a shock for people to realize that life is too short to spend it holding onto grudges.

Making direct amends with the important people in our lives is an integral part of loving others. The gift of love is precious, and it is sometimes only when we risk giving it away by wanting to mend relationships that we really experience the joy of loving. For there is LITTLE RECEIVING WITHOUT THE BRINGING of direct amends.

[1]Ephesians 4:15.
[2]Romans 8:28.

Lord, loving others is such hard work...
It's so easy to give excuses.
It's so easy to be filled with pride.
It's so easy to be dishonest.
It's so easy to be unappreciative.
It's so easy to ignore Your will.

Lord, help me to see that the crux of loving
   is being willing to make amends.

It's willing to be responsible.
It's willing to be humble.
It's willing to be honest.
It's willing to be affirming.
It's willing to be aware of Your will and
   act on it.

For there is little loving without making amends, and
   There is LITTLE RECEIVING WITHOUT THE BRINGING
      of direct amends.
         Amen

Little Life without the Living[1]

*"Jesus said to her,
'Go, call your husband, and come here.'
The woman answered him, 'I have no husband.'
Jesus said to her, 'You are right in saying,
"I have no husband," for you have had five husbands,
and he whom you now have is not your husband;
this you say truly' . . . The woman said to him,
'I know the Messiah is coming (he who is called the Christ);
when he comes, he will show us all things.'
Jesus said to her, 'I who speak to you am he.' . . .
So the woman left her water jar, and went away into the city,
and said to the people, 'Come, see a man who told me
all that I ever did. Can this be the Christ?'
They went out of the city and were coming to him."*

John 4:16-18, 25-26, and 28-30

Knowing the love and forgiveness of the Lord through our relationship with Him and the sharing of ourselves with others can enable us to experience creative transformation. This "spiritual experience is a realization that we are not alone in our difficulties.[2] We recognize that we have achieved a deep awareness of Christ through our self awareness and our relationship with the important others in our life. Because we have found this attitude of joy and gratitude, we

---

[1]This chapter should be read with Step XII of the Twelve Steps for Christian Living: "Having experienced a new sense of spirituality as a result of these steps and realizing that this is a gift of God's grace, we are willing to share the message of His love and forgiveness with others and to practice these principles for spiritual living in all our affairs."

[2]V. Bittner, "Study Guide," *You Can Help with Your Healing*, p. 23.

want to live it out in our relationship with others. We want them, too, to know the transforming friendship of Christ. For there is no life without the living and sharing of what He has done and is doing for us.

The Gift That Never Stops Giving

If you are going to be there for others or be a Christ for others so that they, too, can know His love and joy, you can't just sit and listen with your ears—you have to listen with your heart. The older I get the more I'm aware that we often are saying one thing and feeling another. To really be for others we need to be as non-condemning as Jesus was to the woman "taken in adultery."[1] We must not make judgments, nor censor, nor just listen to the things we want to hear. If we are only going to be advocates of people who have solvable problems or speak only of things that entertain us, then we are denying the truth, and our help will only leave them more alone and more isolated.

There are some people in our society who are called "do-gooders." They are out to SAVE the world. They are fairly good listeners, but they come with an agenda. Unfortunately, it is their agenda and not the person's to whom they are listening. These people give the impression that somehow they are better than the one being listened to, and they convey the idea that the situation they are hearing about could never happen to them.

What they are offering is only sympathy, not empathy. There is a difference! Sympathy conveys that somehow the listener is superior to the one being listened to, and while they try to be loving, their love never seems genuine. Empathy, on the other hand, conveys that we are their equal and that we do understand to some degree how they feel because we know that the situation could have happened to us. Sympathy is often saying, "You poor slob, you can't do it for yourself, so I'll do it for you." And interestingly, they will usually let us do it, just to get us off their backs. But they have missed being given the love of

[1]See Chapter VI.

Christ. If they respond, they are only going through the motions, and then they have given up one bondage for another—being phony. They haven't found the freedom that is available in Jesus Christ by taking the risk of being who they really are.

Empathy, on the other hand, is saying, "but for the grace of God," I too would be where you are. This in no way means that God is more gracious to us than He is to them. It only means that I have not had this misfortune. This attitude lets them know that they are not being judged, but rather that they are being loved in spite of what they have done. People can respond to this, because they are beginning to experience the unconditional love of Christ that has been our experience *if* we have had a spiritual awakening.

There isn't a one of us who is so strong that we could not have been destroyed by some events of life. Therefore, we need to approach those who are feeling alienated with a sense of gratitude and a desire to be understanding. Otherwise, we will be just one more person in a long line of those who only accentuated their loneliness.

And I know this feeling! Most of my life I have felt lonely. This was true partly because I didn't risk intimacy, partly because I never learned how to love, and perhaps partly because this was my condition. Earlier in this book I said that loneliness was a choice, and it is, but for me I think that I would add that loneliness involves YEARNING TO BE UNDERSTOOD, yearning to be understood whether we are "bad" or "good."

There are always people who will love you when you are a success. I was a success, at least in the eyes of the world. Unfortunately, there are few who listen to you or love you when things aren't going right. Most of the time this only merited criticism and a flippant "I told you so." Because I didn't want to hear this I became a perfectionist and I worked hard—so hard that I developed high blood pressure and became a workaholic. Thank God, I woke up to life and started living it. I took care of my blood pressure by losing weight and exercising. And I have now begun with Christ's help to curb my workaholism. For there is LITTLE LIFE WITHOUT THE LIVING, and there is limited life if you spend all your waking moments working.

One of the greatest gifts of life that I have received in recent years is *friendship*. If we really have a friendship, we experience the kind of gift that never stops giving. If we truly experience the creative transformation of Christ, we know what a true transformation is and means, and we want to pass it on. Perhaps the most difficult lesson I have had to learn about friendship is to accept being given to as well as to give. There is little friendship, even with the estranged and the "lost," unless there is both giving and receiving.

In working with hurting people, I find no greater joy than being privileged to share in their life story. How honored I am for them to trust me enough to be so vulnerable. People who are hurting always think that I am doing them such a favor to listen to them, and then I remind them of how *graced* I feel.

Approaching hurting people requires our realizing that through our listening we will be receiving. If we don't realize this, we will be guilty of giving in a way that will please ourselves and will not help them to help themselves. When we don't recognize their gift to us, we revert to our own agenda because we think we are doing them a favor. We fail to see the listening and sharing as a mutual experience of receiving.

The Samaritan Woman

As Christ was sitting at the well, a woman came to draw some water. It wasn't at the usual time. The natural time was in the cool of the evening, when it was customary for all of the women to gather about the well and share the events of the day.

A possible explanation for her coming in the middle of the day was that she was both a Samaritan woman and that she had a bad reputation. As a result, she was unpopular in the town and felt isolated. Rather than endure any possible ridicule, she perhaps had formed a habit of going to the well when it was reasonably certain that she would be the only person there. Anyway, there she was, and Christ was there too. He reached out to her. He asked her for a drink of water.

Maybe what draws most of us to Jesus is not so much what He gives, but rather *what He asks*. So often we refuse what He has to offer us, but we feel energized by the possibility of sharing in His ministry of reconciliation and transformation. Even though we need to accept what He offers, it is sometimes easier to be challenged by what He calls us to do. At least being challenged is a place to start, and as we experience His love more fully by reaching out, we are better able to experience His transforming friendship.

When we respond to His call, we are struck by the mystery of His words, "Inasmuch as you have done it unto the least of these, my brothers and sisters, you did it unto me" (Matthew 25:40). Sometimes it is easier to follow His call and *do* something than it is to *receive* His love. Many times it is easier to get caught up with doing things than it is to accept His love, because love requires a response on our part. It is sometimes less threatening for us to *do* things than it is just to *be*. Then we can justify not allowing the Lord to love us because we are reaching out to the lonely, needy, and down-and-out. Not to say that helping the needy is not admirable, but sometimes we may do this to avoid the penetrating love of Christ, which may force us to look at the things we don't wish to see. Then we can even feel somewhat justified when we reject His unconditional love.

This, I think, is why so many non-Christians are "do-gooders." Rather than be vulnerable enough and humble enough to accept the love of Christ and admit their need for Him, they are trying to save themselves by saving the world, not realizing that sometimes the only way some people find salvation is if they are left to fall to the depths, and also that some people refuse salvation. After all, even Christ couldn't reach some people, and He was perfect. How do such people expect to find salvation? Maybe it is only an ego trip, and their magnanimous acts of kindness are only their way of proving to themselves that they aren't as bad as they once thought. So their compulsion to help the world is their way to vindicate themselves and to continue to deny their need for a Savior, who is Jesus Christ.

But the important point is that Jesus and the Samaritan woman met. After Jesus asks her for a drink, she is amazed. How could He, Jesus, ask her, a Samaritan woman and a person of the street, for anything?

One can hardly understand why Jesus would choose such a person to be the messenger of the fact that He was the Messiah, the Christ. He could have chosen anyone else, but He picked this person who had three strikes against her: She was a woman, a Samaritan, and a sinner.

Most sermonizers jump on the issues that she was LIVING IN SIN. After all, she had had five husbands and was now living with the sixth. One wonders if the sins of the five or six men are even considered. We are told that we have all sinned and "fallen short of the glory of God" (Romans 3:23), and there is no one sin which is worse than another in the eyes of the Lord. Whatever separates us from God, others, and *even ourselves* is sin.

In this account, it is not hard to see how the sexual sin can be the point of emphasis, even though only three verses out of thirty are devoted to her marital status. It is so easy to be critical and judgmental because this view gets us off the hook. However, if we are willing to look at our own sin and accept that we don't have to save ourselves, we are in a better position to see the positive note of this story—that Jesus called the outcasts of society to be His instruments of love and joy. He chose those who were alienated, separated, and isolated. His call was to the strangers of society and those considered to be foolish because they were willing to be fools for Him.

This story of the woman at the well has three scenes. In the first scene, Jesus asks her for a drink of water. Here we see His humanness, and we also see that this woman is no pushover nor is she ignorant of her heritage. In the six exchanges between them, they spend most of the time discussing religion and specifically the differences between the Jewish and Samaritan practices of worship.

There is no doubt that she is skeptical of Jesus. I suspect that she is also somewhat amused because He, a Jew, is speaking to a Samaritan. More important, she is open to the idea that Jesus' water (living water) is special and she knows that the Messiah is expected. She also is smart enough to see that Jesus is prophetic.

In the second scene, the disciples approach Jesus and are somewhat shocked that He is speaking to a woman in the street. It was forbidden by rabbinical law for a man to be speaking to a woman in the street whether the woman was his wife or not. The woman pays no attention to the disciples and is not deterred by their attitude.

Then the woman departs from Jesus. She is so excited that she leaves her jar of water. She goes to the nearby town and begins to tell everyone in sight, "Come, see a man who told me all that I ever did. Can this be the Christ?" And John says that many Samaritans from that city "believed in Him" as a result of her willingness to tell of her encounter with Jesus.

Because Jesus loved her and accepted her as a person of worth, He trusted her with the fact that He was the Christ. She was so overwhelmed with His acceptance and this information that she couldn't contain herself. She became the medium for His message. His forgiving and transforming love made her worthy to go and tell.

The third scene emphasizes the belief of the people. We are told the people were so moved by her story that they not only believed in Jesus but also asked Him to stay with them. "He stayed there two days. And many more believed because of His word" (verses 40-41). John goes on to say that the people believed not only because of her testimony but because they, too, experienced the Christ. They knew for sure that He was the Savior of the world because they also spent time with Him.

What can we say to the fact that Jesus chose a Samaritan woman who was a sinner to be His agent? Did He deliberately choose to give His revelation to a woman? Or did she just happen to be handy and there at the right moment? It is difficult to know, except that I don't think Jesus did anything by chance.

Why didn't He tell one of His disciples that He was the Christ? Why a Samaritan and not a Jew? Why a woman and not a man? Could it be that Jesus chose her because she was different and He knew people would listen to her for just that reason? Certainly she had *entre* to the Samaritans where a Jew would not. But why would the people listen to someone who was considered disreputable?

Perhaps Jesus wanted to show that there is no one, no matter how bad, that cannot have their life transformed by the dynamic of His love. Perhaps He wanted to show that a person's marital history or one's "living in sin" are not barriers to their being creatively transformed to be an instrument of His message of salvation. I am sure Jesus looked beneath the three negatives and saw a person of worth. This is the way He sees us, too. In spite of what we are, He sees our value, and when we come in touch with Him, the hidden, creative part of us is called forth for the Kingdom.

Just as Christ called her, an outcast and a sinner, so He calls us. Once we have known His transforming friendship we will feel compelled to share it with others. The excitement of being loved by Christ, most often through the important others in our lives, compels us to go and tell others that they too might experience the creative transformation of their lives. He calls us, just as He called this woman, to live—to live through Him, with Him, and for Him. For there is little life without the living.

Throughout my life, I have experienced over and over again the fact that all situations and experiences can be opportunities for spiritual growth.[1] No matter how crooked, ugly, and abusive our lives appear to be, Christ in His love can creatively transform us. We only have to admit our need for Him, risk sharing our hidden selves, accept His unconditional forgiveness, and follow His will for our lives.[2]

As I look back on my life, I am overwhelmed with gratitude for the Lord allowing me to experience both the good and the bad. This has resulted in my becoming more aware of what needs to be changed in my life and in the lives of others. Maybe this is why we are here in this world, where sin and hurt and sorrow abound, so that we can experience how Christ's trans-

---

[1]V. Bittner, *Make Your Illness Count*, Augsburg 1976.
[2]The structure for this is contained in the Twelve Steps for Christian Living.

forming love can create beauty out of the beast within us. This is the only way we can deal with the evil within. We cannot remove it or shackle it. We can only be healed and transformed by the creative love of Jesus Christ.

In 1975, while attending an international meeting for pastoral educators in Zurich, Switzerland, I met a woman who suffered at the hands of the Nazis during the second World War. What she told me seemed almost unbelievable. Yet, her response to that abuse was even more unbelievable.

She told how she and her family were arrested because of her nationality. They looted and raided her home. They killed her mother and father. Her brothers were shot in cold blood. She and her other two sisters were forced to prostitute themselves to the soldiers. As the oldest (eighteen), she was "kept" for a time by one of the officers. She was abused verbally, physically, and sexually. His lust and his sadistic behavior seemed bottomless.

Through complying with his demands, she was able to escape from him and found shelter in a German hospital near the front lines. She was put to work as a nurses' aide and forced to care for the people who had destroyed her home, killed her parents and brothers, and raped her and her sisters.

In our talks together at that conference, she spoke of her struggle—her hatred and her attempt at killing that small, weak voice that kept saying, "You are to love your enemies." She realized she couldn't change this hatred herself. She needed the help of Christ. She remembered that as a Christian she was to pray for her enemies.

The thought of this seemed outrageous. How could she pray for a people who had been so cruel? How could Christ expect anyone to do that? And yet He did. His life and teachings were always challenging and stretching people—sometimes beyond where they thought they couldn't go.

The breakthrough of her anger came one night when she was assigned to care for the officers' ward. Her first evening while she was making rounds, the light from her flashlight passed over the face of a man who looked familiar. She stopped abruptly. Could it be him—the man who hurt her so much? She flashed the light directly into his face. There was no doubt. It was him. There lay the man who was responsible for performing all of those horrible acts.

She could tell that he was severely wounded. In fact, he was almost dead. She knew it wouldn't take much to kill him. After all, didn't he kill her loved ones and cause her slowly to die inside? It was a terrible struggle. Why should God do this to her? And then she remembered the words, "Whatever you do to the least of these, my sister/brother, you will do it to me."

How could she kill Christ? How could she kill a man who loved and suffered and died for her? And everyone, no matter how evil, has a Christ within. The trouble is that all of us have difficulty releasing that part of us at times.

Unable to look at the man any longer, she turned and ran, and once she was outside the ward, she burst into tears.

She cried for what seemed like hours. Finally, hearing her sobs, she was quieted by the charge nurse on that floor. They spent a few minutes talking. She was able to share her hatred and what she had almost done. The nurse didn't tell her what to do — she only listened with a compassionate heart.

She left the charge nurse and walked slowly back to the bed of the officer. While standing beside him, she suddenly experienced a bright light shining on her from above. She felt warm and cold all at the same time. It was as though that light penetrated right into her heart, and she began to feel peaceful and calm and her need for revenge disappeared.

That night changed her life. Her hatred was transformed into love. She nursed him back to health. In fact, the doctors marvelled at her care of him and how quickly he recovered.

When the officer was well, the doctors wanted to bring in the nurse who cared for him during the silent hours of the night. When she came to his bed and was introduced as the person who "saved his life," he said, "I think we've met before."

"Yes," she said, "we have met before." When the doctors left the room, he almost shouted at her in a whisper, "Why didn't you kill me?" Calmly she said, "I am a follower of Him who said, 'Love your enemies.'"

She went on to say that her hatred had turned to love. She explained to him her experience of Christ's "light" entering her heart, how once she was filled with rage, how she had prayed for him, and how she knew that loving him was really loving her Lord.

The officer lay silent for a long time. Neither one of them spoke a word but there was much shared. He experienced Christ's love through her love in a way that no words can describe. She loved him, not only for the evil within, but for the good which was about to burst forth.

You may wonder what happened to this officer and this woman. They were married and he went on to study for the ministry. Recently, he retired and they are now living together in East Germany.

Sharing our story of how the Lord has creatively transformed us and how He is continuing to do so is necessary in order for us to experience the abundant life. To share ourselves is to find ourselves. In loving and caring for others, we love and care for ourselves. By loving others, we are not only being humane, but we are experiencing our own humanity through the giving and receiving. By caring for others we are living the abundant life and providing the opportunity for others to be transformed by the love of Christ. For there is little life, LIFE ABUNDANT, without the living. There is little abundant life without LOVING GOD, OURSELF, AND OTHERS.

Lord, I thank You and praise You . . .
for being there for me,
for hearing me when I cry,
for rejoicing when I rejoice,
for answering my prayers,
for loving me so I can love,
and for transforming my life and
continuing to do it in such a creative way.

HELP ME, LORD, TO PASS IT ON!

Amen

Twelve Steps for Christian Living

1. We admit our need for God's gift of salvation, that we are powerless over certain areas of our lives and that our lives are at times sinful and unmanageable.

2. We come to believe through the Holy Spirit that a power who came in the person of Jesus Christ and who is greater than ourselves can transform our weaknesses into strengths.

3. We make a decision to turn our will and our lives over to the care of Christ as we understand Him—hoping to understand Him more fully.

4. We make a searching and fearless moral inventory of ourselves— both our strengths and our weaknesses.

5. We admit to Christ, to ourselves, and to another human being the exact nature of our sins.

6. We become entirely ready to have Christ heal all of these defects of character that prevent us from having a more spiritual lifestyle.[1]

7. We humbly ask Christ to transform all of our shortcomings.[2]

8. We make a list of all persons we have harmed and become willing to make amends to them all.

9. We make direct amends to such persons wherever possible, except when to do so would injure them or others.

10. We continue to take personal inventory and when we are wrong, promptly admit it, and when we are right, thank God for His guidance.

11. We seek through prayer and meditation to improve our conscious contact with Christ as we understand Him, praying for knowledge of His will for us and the power to carry that out.

12. Having experienced a new sense of spirituality as a result of these steps and realizing that this is a gift of God's grace, we are willing to share the message of His love and forgiveness with others and to practice these principles for spiritual living in all our affairs.

[1,2]These two steps have been revised from the original Twelve Steps for Christian Living found in *You Can Help with Your Healing*.

Many people wish to work on their spiritual lives, but they sometimes lack the commitment and the tools to do so. The Twelve Steps for Christian Living as outlined in the book *You Can Help With Your Healing* and the accompanying "Study Guide" provide the structure and planned climate for spiritual growth in the context of a small group.

If you would like more information or a *starter packet* for beginning these groups, write to:

Institute for Christian Living
P. O. Box 22408
Minneapolis, MN   55422

*"You are living a brand new life
that is continually learning more and more
of what is right, and trying constantly
to be more like Christ who created
this new life within you."*

Colossians 3:10, *The Living Bible*